Also by Timothy B. Benford

The World War II Quiz & Fact Book (Volume 1)
Hitler's Daughter, a novel

THE
WORLD WAR II
QUIZ & FACT
BOOK VOLUME 2

TIMOTHY B. BENFORD

1817

HARPER & ROW, PUBLISHERS, New York

*Cambridge, Philadelphia, San Francisco, London
Mexico City, São Paulo, Sydney*

For Marilyn, again

FIRST EDITION

Library of Congress Cataloging in Publication Data
(Revised for vol. 2)

Benford, Timothy B.
  The World War II quiz & fact book.

  Includes bibliographies and indexes.
  1. World War, 1939-1945 — Miscellanea. I. World War
II quiz & fact book. II. World War 2 quiz and fact book.
III. World War two quiz and fact book. IV. Title.
D743.9.B464 1982   940.53   82-47516
ISBN 0-06-015025-4 (v. 1)
ISBN 0-06-090978-1 (pbk. : v. 1)
ISBN 0-06-015284-2 (v. 2)   84 85 86 87 88 10 9 8 7 6 5 4 3 2 1
ISBN 0-06-091136-0 (pbk. : v. 2)   84 85 86 87 88 10 9 8 7 6 5 4 3 2 1

Contents

Introduction

As I noted in what has now become Volume 1 of *The World War II Quiz & Fact Book,* there was never a problem of what to include. I also noted that space simply did not permit the use of all the information. The problem was, and still is, what *not* to put in.

The war years, and in some cases events that followed but are directly related, remain full of historic treasures, bits of information, nostalgia, anecdotes, vignettes, all scattered throughout the millions of printed pages of war books. But the wealth of information does not end there.

Since publication of the first volume in December 1982, I have had the privilege of meeting and communicating with literally hundreds of veterans who have offered nuggets of their own. Most were Americans, but there have been many Canadians and Britons and a few French, Japanese and Germans also.

There was tremendous interest in the Naval section and the attack on Pearl Harbor. Code names and nicknames were equally popular, while most people were not too keen on bothering to remember specific dates. Consequently I have organized the material in this volume to reflect those preferences.

The Air and Land sections in this volume are as strong as in the first. Messages and Quotations, on the other hand, is smaller only because by now I may have exhausted the majority of truly memorable utterances.

For the reader seeing this work without having previously read the original volume, I hasten to note that each volume can be enjoyed without the other. There is no continuity lost, as the material skips over the period without regard to chronology.

However, occasionally I have supplied parenthetical references to specific pages in Volume 1. Their only purpose is to call attention to additional information about a particular person or event in case the reader cares to know more.

In the first volume I depended heavily upon photographs from official sources. I am delighted to note that this volume also has a generous selection of photographs taken by individuals who were kind enough to permit me to reproduce them. For the most part these were snapshots privately taken by service personnel. Three of the photo contributors, however, were wartime photographers in the Signal Corps. Appropriate credit lines are included for all photos, official and private.

Every effort has been made to publish only information that I was able to confirm from at least two other printed sources. The bibliography for this work, as with the last, is in excess of one hundred books. But if the reader discovers an error, it must be mine alone.

TIMOTHY B. BENFORD

Mountainside, New Jersey
August 1983

Posterity!! You will never know how much it cost the present generation to preserve your freedom. I hope you will make good use of it.

—U.S. President John Adams
1797

Q. What was the name of General Douglas MacArthur's private B-17?
A. *Bataan.* In the top photo, MacArthur and Admiral Thomas Kinkaid discuss the war as the general's plane wings toward New Guinea on February 27, 1944. In the bottom photo Lieutenant General Robert L. Eichelberger, commanding general of the U.S. Eighth Army, sits near the waist gun in his B-17, *Miss Em*, during a flight from Leyte to Mindoro, Philippines, on March 17, 1945.

Code Names

Q. What was the German code name for the plan to assassinate President Franklin D. Roosevelt?

A. Operation Long Pounce, which was said to be scheduled for execution during the Teheran Conference.

Q. What was the name Adolf Hitler used to avoid being recognized before his face was so widely known?

A. Herr Wolf.

Q. What was the Allied code name for Guadalcanal?

A. Cactus. (Volume 1, page 40)

Q. What was the name Nazi Rudolf Hess gave to authorities after his dramatic flight to and capture in Scotland on May 10, 1941?

A. Alfred Horn. Hess, who was at the time the third-highest-ranking Nazi behind Hitler and Goering, was still a prisoner in Spandau Prison, Germany, as 1983 ended.

Q. General James M. Gavin was known as
      a. Bad Jim
      b. Big Jim
      c. Slim Jim
      d) Jumpin' Jim

A. He was more commonly known as Slim Jim, but Jumpin' Jim was also a name he earned. (Volume 1, page 121)

Q. Who were the Devil's Brigade?
A. U.S. and Canadian troops under the command of U.S. General
   Robert T. Frederick that used unconventional tactics against the
   Axis forces in Italy. They were officially known as the First Special
   Service Force.

Q. Who were the Hell's Angels?
A. It was the name of a squadron of Flying Tigers that included the
   youngest and first member of the Flying Tigers killed in action,
   twenty-one-year-old Henry Gilbert. He was shot down over Rangoon
   in December 1941.

Q. What was Hell's Highway?
A. The road captured by the U.S. 82nd and 101st Airborne Divisions
   in Holland during Operation Market Garden. More than 20,000
   Allied troops participated in the drops intended to outflank the
   Siegfried Line and push into the Ruhr basin.

Q. What did U.S. bomber pilots call the Happy Valley?
A. The Ruhr Valley in Germany earned the name because of the heavy
   anti-aircraft guns there.

Q. What did Allied pilots nickname the flight path between airfields
   in the Marianas Islands and Tokyo, Japan?
A. Hirohito Highway.

Q. Identify the air route nicknamed the Aluminum Trail.
A. The aircraft run over the Himalayas to China. The dubious distinction was a testimony to the several planes that never completed
   the flight.

Q. What was the name given to the Allied supply route from Antwerp,
   Belgium, to the northern battlefronts in Europe?
A. The ABC Express, not to be confused with the Red Ball Express,
   which was the route for supplies from the Normandy beaches inland.

Q. Which unit was known as the Black Bulls?
A. The British 79th Armoured Division.

Q. Identify the spy Ian Fleming is said to have used as a model for James Bond, the character in the novel and film series.

A. Fleming, who was a British intelligence agent himself, is said to have based his fictional agent on the life of a key double agent under his charge, Dusko Popov. Popov, who died at age seventy in France in 1981, published his memoirs, *Spy-Counterspy*, in 1974.

Q. What was British Prime Minister Winston Churchill's code name for telephone calls to U.S. President Franklin D. Roosevelt?
　　a. Colonel Warden
　　b. Former Naval Person
　　c. John Martin

A. He was John Martin on the phone, Former Naval Person in written communication with FDR and Colonel Warden in British military and diplomatic codes. (Volume 1, pages 34 and 45)

Q. What was the special attachment U.S. and RAF crews had for the Gibson Girl?

A. It was a vital part of their survival equipment. A radio transmitter that broadcast SOS messages, it saved the lives of numerous aircrews shot down over water.

Q. Who was Josip Broz?

A. Better known as Tito, he was head of the resistance forces (communist) in Yugoslavia.

Q. Which U.S. general had a Piper Cub named the *Missouri Mule*?
　　a. Dwight D. Eisenhower
　　b. Douglas MacArthur
　　c. Omar Bradley
　　d. George C. Marshall

A. General Omar Bradley.

FACT Ian Fleming, author of the James Bond series, named his estate on the Caribbean island of Jamaica Golden Eye after the war. He took the name from British Prime Minister Winston Churchill's plan to secure Gibraltar if the Spanish had joined the Axis in the war. Fleming, as a member of the British intelligence system, was involved in the plan. (Volume 1, page 162)

Q. Who was Max Heilinger?

A. It was the fictitious name the SS used to establish a bank account in which they deposited money, gold and jewels taken from European Jews.

Q. What was Klim?

A. Milk, backwards. It was the powdered milk U.S. troops learned to live with.

Q. What was Meyer's Hunting Horn?

A. The name Berliners gave to air-raid sirens. Hermann Goering, who was among other things Chief Huntsman and Game Warden of the Reich, had once said that if Allied bombs fell on Germany people could call him Meyer.

Q. What did Hitler intend to rename Berlin after its planned modernization by architect Albert Speer?
- a. Teutonia
- b. Germania
- c. Europa

A. Germania.

Q. What were the Japanese "windship weapons"?

A. The paper balloons and rubberized-silk balloons that Japan launched against the northwestern U.S. The first of more than 9,000 balloons carrying incendiary and anti-personnel bombs was launched on November 3, 1944. Six Americans were killed, and the balloons reached as far east as Michigan. The Smithsonian Institution has one of the paper versions on display. It was recovered at Echo, Oregon, on March 13, 1945.

Q. What was the most powerful artillery gun created by any nation and used in the war?

A. A monstrous gun developed by the Germans that could project a 2½-ton shell over three miles. The shells, twenty-four inches wide, were capable of going through eight to nine feet of concrete. Nicknamed Karl after its designer, General Karl Becker, the gun was used against the Russians.

USIS Photo

Q. What was the name of Edward R. Murrow's radio program from London?

A. *London After Dark*. (Volume 1, page 130)

Q. Who were the BAMs?

A. The U.S. Marine Corps simply called females in its ranks Women Marines. However, not wanting to be outdone by WACs, WAVES, WAFs and WASPs, some enterprising leathernecks coined the term BAMs — which stood for Broad-Assed Marines. The women, however, called the men HAMs, or Hairy-Assed Marines.

Q. What was the name of Bill Mauldin's jeep, which he converted into a mobile art studio?

A. Mauldin, the creator of "Willie and Joe," dubbed the jeep *Jeanie*.

Q. What did U.S. Admiral Chester Nimitz name his jeep?

A. USS *Hush Hush*. In Navy tradition it was painted battleship gray.

Q. Name the popular U.S. general who used a C-47 plane named *Mary Q*.

A. Omar Bradley.

Q. President Franklin D. Roosevelt's private plane, a C-87, was named:
    a. France
    b. Commando
    c. Sacred Cow
    d. Jingle Jangle

A. FDR's plane was the *Sacred Cow*. French General Charles de Gaulle's C-56 was *France* and British Prime Minister Winston Churchill's LB-30 was *Commando*. Elliott Roosevelt, the President's son, piloted a B-17 named *Jingle Jangle*.

FACT Nazi propagandists took full advantage of the name a U.S. B-17 bomber crew had given their plane and had painted on their jackets. When they were forced to bail out over Germany and were captured, the Nazis released stories that the U.S. Army Air Force was employing Chicago gangsters to bomb German cities. The name of the plane, and on the flight jackets, was *Murder Inc.*

Q. The German code name for the plan to infiltrate Allied lines in U.S. uniforms during the Battle of the Bulge was the same as the code name Erwin Rommel gave to his command car in North Africa. What was it?
      a. Grief
      b. Chaos
      c. Surprise

A. Operation Grief, which initially disrupted U.S. forces but did not accomplish the amount of harm the Germans expected.

Q. What was the name of Benito Mussolini's horse?
A. The Duce's white stallion was named Atlantico.

Q. What was the name of U.S. General Jonathan Wainwright's horse?
A. Joseph Conrad. When food supplies had been exhausted on Bataan in 1942, U.S. troops ate the horse.

Q. Match these leaders with the names of their private trains:
      a) General Alfred Jodl   *Bayonet*
      b) Adolf Hitler   *Steiermark*
      c) Hermann Goering   *Asia*
      d) General Dwight D. Eisenhower   *Atlas*
      e) Heinrich Himmler   *Amerika*

A. Jodl had *Atlas*; Hitler rode in *Amerika*; Goering preferred *Asia*; Ike picked *Bayonet*; and Himmler's was *Steiermark*.

Q. What was the name of Adolf Hitler's yacht?
A. *Grille*.

Q. Who was known as the Rommel of the jungle?
A. Japanese General Tomoyuki Yamashita, because of his dynamic and resourceful leadership. Unlike Rommel, however, he managed also to gain a reputation for cruelty.

FACT At the outbreak of war the U.S. was the only major power that did not have an organized intelligence operation.

Q. What was the name of the brothel the SS ran for foreign diplomats and other VIP's in Berlin?

A. The Kitty Salon.

Q. What were Liberty Steaks?

A. The popular hamburger, which was renamed as a home-front propaganda move in the U.S. to avoid having to call them what sounded distinctly German.

Q. Identify the U.S. Army Air Force unit that was nicknamed the Forgotten Air Force.

A. Because they felt the U.S. Eighth Army Air Force received all the glory and publicity, the troops in the Fifteenth Army Air Force gave themselves the nickname.

Q. Identify the two code names used for the British operation to employ a look-alike for Field Marshal Bernard Law Montgomery.

A. Operation Hambone and Operation Copperhead. The individual selected was an actor, E. Clifton-James, who later wrote a book about his role and portrayed himself in the movie *I Was Monty's Double*. Fellow actor Colonel David Niven solicited Clifton-James for the job. The ruse was terminated when the actor had a difficult time giving up tobacco and alcohol. Monty didn't smoke or drink.

Q. What popular song had the Germans rewritten the words for and played over the air for Allied troops to hear less than forty-eight hours before the Normandy landings?

A. "I Double Dare You." The new lyrics read, in part: "I double dare you to venture too near...I double dare you to try and invade."

Q. The trio of Sherman tanks, under the command of Captain Raymond Dronne, that were the first Allied tanks to enter Paris in 1944 were named after Napoleon's battles. Name them.

A. The tanks, which clanked along the same route that Bonaparte had taken in his return from Elba, were *Montmirail, Romilly* and *Champaubert*. Their arrival within the city limits of Paris was on August 24, 1944. In photo at left, the first tank passes through the Porte d'Italie (the Italian Door) entrance to the city.

Metro Photo

Q. Identify the U.S. song whose music was pirated by the Nazis for their "Sieg Heil" march.
A. The Harvard "Fight" song.

Q. Name the popular song written on December 7, 1941, by Charles Tobias and Clifford Friend.
A. "We Did It Before (and We Can Do It Again)."

Q. Identify the Swedish female singer who was known as the voice of Lili Marlene to both the Allied and Axis troops.
A. Lala Andersen, who sang in Berlin cabarets during the war years. (Volume 1, page 87)

Q. Name the female singer known to British troops as the Forces' Sweetheart.
A. Vera Lynn. Her theme song was "We'll Meet Again."

Q. Identify the U.S. entertainer nicknamed the Allied V-2.
A. Dinah Shore. The name stuck after a reporter called her a bombshell.

Q. Who was known as Miss Spark Plug?
A. U.S. Army Colonel Oveta Culp Hobby, commander of the WACs.

Q. Name the woman who was known as the Mother of the WAVES.
A. Senator Margaret Chase Smith, who was one of the prime supporters of a more active role for women in the U.S. Navy.

Q. What was the name of the children's section of the Communist movement in Italy?
A. Koba, which was Joseph Stalin's childhood nickname.

FACT In May 1982, ABC News broadcast evidence that a Soviet code book found on a Finnish battlefield after World War II permitted the U.S. to break the Soviet spy codes. It was information gained from this effort that led the FBI to put Ethel and Julius Rosenberg under surveillance, but this fact was not revealed, since the U.S. didn't want the Soviets to know it had broken the codes. The Rosenbergs were convicted and executed in 1951 for espionage.

Q. Identify the Allied campaign that German propaganda radio broadcaster Axis Sally derided by calling it "the largest self-supporting prisoner-of-war camp in the world."

A. Mildred E. Gillars, known as Axis Sally, used the expression to underscore the inability of the Allies to break out from the beaches of Anzio, Italy, for a considerable time after the initial invasion. (Volume 1, pages 35 and 129)

Q. Besides Axis Sally, another female propaganda broadcaster for the Nazis was:
> a. Stuttgart Steffie
> b. Nuremberg Nancy
> c. Berlin Betty
> d. Luftwaffe Lucy

A. Berlin Betty, whose voice became well known to Allied troops in North Africa.

Q. Who was the Nazi propaganda broadcaster known as Mr. O.K.?

A. Max O. Koischwitz, a naturalized U.S. citizen who returned to Germany in 1939 but never quite gained the notoriety of William Joyce, Lord Haw Haw.

Q. Who was known as the Humbug of Hamburg?
> a. Joseph Goebbels
> b. Hermann Goering
> c. William Joyce (Lord Haw Haw)

A. The name belonged to William Joyce, an American-born British subject who broadcast propaganda for Germany. (Volume 1, page 35)

Q. Who was Lady Haw Haw?

A. German propaganda broadcaster Jane Anderson. Born in America, she was active in both the Spanish Civil War and the first 2½ years of World War II.

Q. Who was known as the Most Feared Man in Europe?

A. German super commando Otto Skorzeny. (Volume 1, page 80)

FACT The Wehrmacht used a delousing powder that was named Russia.

Q. Who was known as the Bitch of Buchenwald?

A. Ilse Koch, wife of Karl Koch, commandant of the Büchenwald concentration camp from 1937 to 1942. She was convicted of crimes against humanity for her part in several tortures and murders. She committed suicide while in a German prison during the mid-1960s while serving a life sentence for war crimes.

Q. Who was the Beast of Belsen?

A. Josef Kramer, commander of the concentration camp, who was executed for crimes against humanity.

Q. Who was known as the Angel of Death of Auschwitz?

A. Dr. Josef Mengele, who performed a variety of experiments on human beings with little regard for their pain or suffering. His present whereabouts, like that of Martin Bormann, remains a mystery.

Q. Identify the European Resistance movement leader known as the King of Shadows.

A. Frenchman Jean Moulin, because of his ability to appear and vanish in the dark of night. (Volume 1, page 81)

Q. Who was nicknamed the Fuehrer's Fireman?

A. Field Marshal Walther Model. He earned the name as a result of Hitler repeatedly giving him charge of difficult situations.

Q. Identify the high-ranking Nazi nicknamed the Flying Tailor by other Nazis.

A. Because of his large wardrobe of uniforms, Reichsmarschall Hermann Goering earned the name.

Q. Name the Luftwaffe fighter ace known as the Star of Africa.

A. Jans J. Marseille, who is credited with scoring seventeen enemy "kills" in a single day. His total was 158.

FACT Actor John Banner, who is best known for his portrayal of Sergeant Schultz in the television series *Hogan's Heroes*, was a Jew who left Austria after the Nazis took over the country in 1938. During the war he posed for U.S. recruiting posters.

Q. Identify the German fighter ace known as the Blond Knight.
A. The ace of aces, of all nations, Erich Hartmann, with 352 "kills."
(Volume 1, page 214)

Q. Who was known as the Iron Man of Malta?
A. Canadian fighter ace George F. Beurling, who scored thirty-one
"kills." Twenty-nine of them were earned when Malta was cited as
the "most bombed spot on earth."

Q. Identify the U.S. Army Air Force unit known as the Flying
Buccaneers.
A. Established on February 5, 1942, under the command of Lieuten-
ant General George C. Kenney, the Fifth Army Air Force was the
Flying Buccaneers.

Q. Who were the Flying Knights?
A. The squadron of P-38s under the command of Major Richard I. Bong
in the Fifth Army Air Force. Bong was the top U.S. ace of the war
with forty "kills."

Q. Who were the Lone Eagles?
A. The members of the all-black 99th Pursuit Fighter Squadron.

Q. Identify the homosexual member of Adolf Hitler's inner circle who
was called "Fraulein Anna" by others in the group.
A. Deputy Fuehrer Rudolf Hess, who was also known as the Brown
Mouse. (Volume 1, pages 106, 144 and 195)

Q. Who were known as Iron Ass and Stone Ass?
A. General Curtis LeMay was the former while V. M. Molotov was the
latter.

FACT On June 24, 1947, a Boise, Idaho, businessman named Kenneth
Arnold sighted what he described as unidentified flying objects
that looked like "pie plates skipping over the water" near Mount
Rainier, Washington. Newspaper reporters coined the term "flying saucers." However, Allied pilots reported similar sightings
during the war, and these UFO's were known as foo-fighters.
Pilots reporting them were often removed from flight duty.

Q. Identify the U.S. ship known as the Ship That Wouldn't Die.

A. The aircraft carrier USS *Franklin* (CV-13) earned the name as a result of surviving the third-greatest U.S. naval disaster ever, yet managing to travel some 12,000 miles from the coast of Japan to Brooklyn Navy Yard for repairs. More than 830 crewmen died as a result of the March 19, 1945, battle off Japan. The greatest single loss of U.S. Navy personnel (1,177) at one time was aboard the USS *Arizona* (BB-39) at Pearl Harbor. The greatest single loss of U.S. Navy personnel at sea was the sinking of the USS *Indianapolis* (nearly 900 lives), on July 30, 1945. (Volume 1, page 114)

Q. Which U.S. aircraft carrier was known as the Blue Ghost?

A. The USS *Lexington* (CV-16), which was launched five weeks after her namesake (CV-2) was sunk. The nickname came about from the fact that she was not painted in a camouflage pattern.

Q. Name the ship known as the Galloping Ghost of the Java Coast.

A. The heavy cruiser USS *Houston*, which was reported sunk twice by the Japanese, including once in the Battle of the Java Sea. She was finally sunk on March 1, 1942, along with the Australian cruiser HMAS *Perth*, in Sunda Strait.

Q. Identify the U.S. ship nicknamed the Galloping Ghost of the Oahu Coast.

A. Also known as the Old Lady and the Big E, the aircraft carrier USS *Enterprise* (CV-6) enjoyed the nickname. After the war the *Enterprise* remained in the mothball fleet stationed at Bayonne, New Jersey. She made her last sea voyage from the Brooklyn Navy Yard to the former Federal Shipyard in Kearny, New Jersey, on August 22, 1958, where she was cut up for scrap after having been sold for $561,333. Efforts to convert the ship into a memorial, under the direction of Admiral William F. Halsey, were unsuccessful.

Q. What was Operation Magic Carpet?

A. The name given to the U.S. operation to return overseas personnel to the United States at the end of the war. The ships involved were called the Magic Carpet Fleet. Scenes such as the one at left were eagerly awaited in all theaters of the war.

Exclusive Photo by Joseph De Caro

Q. Which U.S. unit was nicknamed the Ghost Corps?
A. The U.S. XX Corps, Third Army.

Q. Which ship was known as the First Lady of the Third Fleet?
A. The 52,000-ton battleship USS *Iowa* (BB-61).

Q. Identify the U.S. Navy officer nicknamed the Oil King of the Pacific for his ability to supply ships.
A. Commodore Augustine H. Gray.

Q. Identify the ship known as the Fightingest Ship in the Royal Canadian Navy.
A. Commissioned in August 1943, the Canadian destroyer HMCS *Haida* saw action in the English Channel and the Bay of Biscay. She is credited with destroying fourteen enemy ships. She is now a memorial open to the public at Ontario, Canada.

Q. Identify the naval engagement that is called the Japanese Pearl Harbor.
A. The U.S. attack against the Japanese at Truk on February 16–17, 1944. American planes, based on aircraft carriers, inflicted serious damage on the Japanese. However, the heaviest Japanese ships lost in the strike were light cruisers (*Naga* and *Agano*) and a training cruiser (*Katori*). The *Agano* was actually sunk by a U.S. submarine.

Q. What was known as the Concrete Battleship?
A. U.S. Fort Drum in Manila Bay, the Philippines. It was located approximately five miles from Corregidor.

Q. What four detachments were identified by the code names Concrete, Granite, Iron and Steel during one of history's most daring assaults in May 1940?
A. The four detachments that assaulted the Belgian Fort Eben Emael. (Volume 1, page 125)

FACT William Hitler, a nephew of Adolf Hitler, was in the U.S. Navy during the war. He changed his name upon returning to the U.S. after the war.

Q. Identify the U.S. Navy ship nicknamed the Pirate of the Pacific.

A. The USS *Kidd* (DD-661), which was commissioned in April 1943. After reaching the eastern Pacific, she participated in every major naval campaign until the end of the war, and is now on public view as a memorial in Baton Rouge, Louisiana.

Q. Name "the ship that was always there."

A. The slogan, and reputation, belonged to the battleship USS *Washington* (BB-56), which won thirteen battle stars in the war.

Q. Identify the ship known as Battleship X until information about her joining the fleet had been declassified.

A. The USS *South Dakota* (BB-57).

Q. Identify the U.S. aircraft carrier known as the Old Covered Wagon.

A. The USS *Langley* (CV-1), which was converted into a seaplane tender.

Q. What was the nickname of the aircraft carrier USS *Lexington* (CV-2)?

A. Lady Lex. She was the first U.S. aircraft carrier lost in the war, sunk by friendly fire after being badly damaged in the Battle of the Coral Sea in May 1942.

Q. What was the French luxury liner *Normandie* renamed after it was seized by the U.S.?

A. The S.S. *Lafayette*. However, it burned at dockside in New York in February 1942 and had to be scrapped.

Q. Which U.S. ship was known as the Sweet Pea?

A. The USS *Portland* (CA-33), a veteran of twenty-four major actions against Japan. She was also the first ship in the U.S. Navy to carry that city's name.

FACT In a classic case of mistaken identity, shipments of wartime materiel destined for Milne Bay, New Guinea, wound up being sent to Fall River, Massachusetts, where they remained unaccounted for for a considerable time. The code name for Milne Bay was Fall River.

Q. Which U.S. Navy vessel was nicknamed the One-Ship Fleet?
A. The cruiser USS *Salt Lake City*, because of her many single engagements of the enemy in the Pacific.

Q. Identify the U.S. Navy vessels known as mosquito boats.
A. The name applied to PT boats. The Japanese referred to them as Green Dragons.

Q. Which two Japanese ships were the Green Dragon and the Flying Dragon?
A. Two of the six aircraft carriers that took part in the attack on Pearl Harbor, *Soryu* and *Hiryu*, respectively.

Q. What was the nickname of the U.S. submarine USS *Jack*?
A. Jack the Tanker Killer, because she sank four enemy tankers in a single day.

Q. General Pershing was nicknamed Black Jack in World War I. Name the U.S. admiral given the same nickname in World War II.
A. Admiral Frank (Black Jack) Fletcher.

Q. During the German occupation what were the cut-in-half taxis drawn by humans or horses in Paris called?
A. Velo-Taxis. Usually the driver pulled the vehicle by using a bike.

Q. Identify the plane known by Luftwaffe and RAF pilots alike as Goering's Folly.
A. The Messerschmitt BF-110, a twin-engine fighter that was too slow to compete with British fighters.

FACT During the Battle of the Bulge, U.S. General Omar Bradley was challenged by American troops on the lookout for Germans dressed in U.S. uniforms. He was asked to name the capital of Illinois, and correctly responded "Springfield"; the scrimmage position of a guard in football, to which he replied, "Between the center and tackle." However, on three separate challenges he failed to identify the husband of pinup girl and movie star Betty Grable. Despite not knowing that it was bandleader Harry James, Bradley was given passage.

Q. What was the name of the secret road constructed to transport tanks and armor to the hills above Cassino, Italy?
A. Cavendish Road.

Q. What were the GI Joe Diners?
A. Food and rest stops along U.S. supply routes in Europe where canned rations could be exchanged for hot meals.

Q. What was the name of the powder explosive developed by the Allies that could actually be mixed with water, baked and eaten?
A. Because of its strong resemblance to flour and its ability to be digested, in necessity, it was known as Aunt Jemima, with a bow to the famous pancake mix.

Q. What was the code name for the U.S. invasion of Okinawa on April 1, 1945?
A. Operation Iceberg. (Volume 1, pages 132, 134, 157, 179, 186 and 205)

Q. What was the U.S. code name for the invasion of Iwo Jima in 1945?
A. Operation Detachment. (Volume 1, pages x, 3, 27, 60, 85, 125 and 135)

Q. What was the code name for the U.S. Second Marine Division assault on Tarawa in November 1943?
       a. Operation Long Bow
       b. Operation Long Arm
       c. Operation Long Legs
       d. Operation Longsuit
A. Operation Longsuit. (Volume 1, pages 45, 69, 83 and 118)

Q. Who was the individual credited with the actual breakthrough that resulted in the U.S. reading of the Japanese Purple Code?
A. While Colonel William F. Friedman is generally regarded as the individual most responsible for breaking the Purple Code (after nearly twenty months of work), it was the genius of a civilian cryptanalyst, Harry Larry Clark, who triggered the actual breakthrough.

FACT Mikado, Michigan, changed its name to MacArthur, Michigan, after the Japanese attack on Pearl Harbor.

Q. Who advised the Japanese that the U.S. was reading their code messages?

A. Nazi Heinrich Stahmer, the individual who had been entrusted by Hitler to negotiate the Tripartite Pact in Tokyo. Stahmer passed this information on to the Japanese Foreign Ministry in May 1941, but Japan could not believe it possible and, therefore, did not change the codes.

Q. What was the Mechelen Incident?

A. It relates to partially burned documents that outlined German intentions against Belgium. A German plane lost its way on January 10, 1940, and crashed in Belgium. The information salvaged confirmed the thrust intended against the British and French expeditionary forces. Had the Allies fully believed the documents, Germany's advances could have been stopped cold.

Q. What was the name of the German plan to seize the Suez Canal?

A. Part of the overall German objective to take Egypt, the plan was Operation Aida.

Q. What was the Knutsford Affair?

A. The name given to the incident in which U.S. General George S. Patton referred to the U.S. and British destinies to "rule the world" and thereby offended our French and Russian allies.

Q. Who were the Jedburghs?

A. The special teams of one American, a Briton and a Frenchman who worked with the French Maquis.

Q. What was Sho-Go, the Japanese plan for Operation Victory?

A. The plan for crushing any Allied attempt to retake the Philippines.

Q. What was the code name for British General Bernard Montgomery's Lightfoot operations in North Africa during 1942?
  a. Old Bailey
  b. Bertram
  c. Big Ben
A. It was Operation Bertram, the El Alamein offensive. Here a German tank crew surrenders as infantry rush their tank during the campaign.

Imperial War Museum Photo

Q. Name the plane commanded by USAAF Captain Ted Lawson in Doolittle's raid.

A. The *Ruptured Duck*. Lawson wrote the best-selling book *Thirty Seconds over Tokyo*.

Q. Which Allied invasion beaches were code-named Cent, Dime and Joss?
> a. Guadalcanal
> b. Okinawa
> c. Sicily

A. Sicily. Okinawa beaches were Blue and Purple, and Red was the code name for Guadalcanal. Other invasions that had Red beaches include Attu, Dieppe, Saipan, Salerno and Tarawa, either as single objectives or part of a multibeach invasion. (Volume 1, pages 45 and 76)

Q. What was Operation Red?

A. The second and final phase of the German Battle for France. It began as the Dunkirk evacuation ended.

Q. Name the German plan to kidnap Marshal Tito in 1944.

A. Operation Knight's Move, which employed commandos in gliders who swept in but failed to get him.

Q. What was the code name for the U.S. plan to reach Hechingen, Germany, and capture as many German atomic scientists as possible before any of the other Allies?

A. Operation Humbug.

Q. What was the name of the German scheme to counterfeit British currency and bank notes?

A. Operation Bernhard. It was the brainchild of Alfred Naujocks, the SS officer who was in command of the fabricated incident at Gleiwitz, Poland, which the Nazis used as a reason for invading Poland. (Volume 1, page 79)

FACT The French forces under De Gaulle, which had been known as the Free French, were renamed the Fighting French in mid-July 1942.

Q. What was the Italian three-ton light tank (L-3-33/5) irreverently called? (Note: this is the tank that Franco's troops used in the Spanish Civil War and the Italians used unsuccessfully in Libya.)

A. Sardine Can. It was no match for the most modest anti-tank weapons.

Q. What were *grilles de Cointets*?

A. Mobile metal tank traps, named after their inventor, which were designed to assist the Allies during the campaign in Europe prior to Dunkirk.

Q. What term did British Prime Minister Neville Chamberlain use to describe the lull between the declarations of war in September 1939 and open hostilities in the spring of 1940?

A. To Chamberlain it was the Twilight War, while in Germany it was known as the Sitting War (Sitzkrieg).

Q. Who is credited with coining the phrase Phony War?
      a. Winston S. Churchill
      b. William Borah
      c. George S. Patton
      d. Joseph Goebbels

A. U.S. Senator William Borah used the term to describe the period after the European Allies declared war on Germany in September 1939 and the lull that followed until hostilities broke out on a large scale in the spring of 1940.

Q. What was the German code name for the plan to annex the unoccupied area of France after the armistice?

A. Attila.

Q. What was Operation Titanic?

A. The code name for the Allied airborne deception tactics during the D-Day invasion.

FACT Germany benefited greatly from the Phony War inasmuch as by May 10, 1940, when open hostilities broke out, it had mustered 157 divisions. This was forty-nine more than it had on September 1, 1939, when it invaded Poland.

Q. Identify the participants involved in a May 1940 conversation between France and London which was conducted in Hindustani to prevent the Germans from monitoring it.

A. Prime Minister Winston Churchill ordered General Ismay to telephone London and request the Cabinet meet at once to consider a telegram he was sending dealing with continued aid to the French. Ismay arranged for an Indian Army officer to deliver the unusual message. Churchill and Ismay were among a British group in France conducting strategy meetings.

Q. What was known as the German Pak?

A. The term is an abbreviation of *Panzerabwehrkanon*, or anti-tank gun. Anti-tank crews were referred to as Panzerjaeger (tank hunters), which gave an offensive psychological name to a defensive force.

Q. What was the German nickname for the dive-bombing aircraft known as *Sturzkampfflugzeug*?

A. The Junkers Ju-87 was known by both the Allies and the Axis as the Stuka, which is an abbreviation of the German word for dive bomber.

Q. Who was General John C. H. "Courthouse" Lee?

A. Deputy commander under General Dwight D. Eisenhower for European Theater of Operations (ETOUSA).

Q. What was Operation Aphrodite?

A. The secret mission in which Lieutenant Joseph P. Kennedy, Jr. was killed. The objective was to destroy German submarine pens at St. Nazaire and Lorient on the French coast. (Volume 1, page 89)

FACT Elizabeth Windsor, an eighteen-year-old member of the British Auxiliary Territorial Service in 1944, was an automobile mechanic who had a trick played on her by His Majesty King George VI. The King had removed the distributor from a car that the young woman was attempting to get started as part of her final test in a heavy mechanics course. He finally told her the reason she had been unsuccessful and she easily passed the test. Second Subaltern Elizabeth Alexandra Mary Windsor is better known to the world today as Queen Elizabeth II.

Q. Identify the U.S. official who was code-named Mary by the Germans.
   a. William Donovan
   b. Harry Hopkins
   c. Charles A. Lindbergh
A. Wild Bill Donovan, head of the OSS.

Q. What other code name, besides Valkyrie, was the plan to kill Adolf Hitler known by?
A. The July 20, 1944, plot was also called Malaparte. (Volume 1, pages 53 and 85)

Q. What was the German code name for the attack against the Soviets at the Kursk salient in July 1943?
A. Operation Citadel, which resulted in the largest tank and armored battle in history. More than 3,600 tanks and armored vehicles were involved.

Q. What was the name of the British-inspired plan to deceive the Germans as to where the Allies would land during Operation Overlord?
A. Operation Bodyguard, which was intended to convince the Germans that the invasion would be at Calais rather than Normandy.

Q. What was the objective of Operation Dracula?
A. The Allied capture of Rangoon in May 1945.

Q. What was Operation Strangle?
A. The air support that the Allies employed prior to Operation Diadem in an effort to sever German supply routes around Rome. (Volume 1, page 53)

Q. What was the code name for the German effort to land spies in New York and other areas of the U.S. in 1942?
A. Operation Pegasus.

FACT To confuse Japanese who were listening to U.S. Marine Corps radio transmissions in the Pacific during the war, the Corps employed more than 300 Navajo-speaking American Indians as radio code talkers.

Q. What was the German code name for the plan that led to the creation of the Afrika Korps?

A. Operation Sunflower (Sunnenblume). It was intended to use a German force to defend Tripoli.

Q. What was Operation Shoestring?

A. The unofficial name U.S. Marines gave to the Guadalcanal campaign because of the severe shortages of supplies, particularly as they were required by Marine Corps Aviation.

Q. Identify the code name for the British plan to keep the 7th Australian Division in the Nile delta for a possible attack on Rhodes and Leros, Greece.

A. Operation Mandible.

Q. What was the Allied code name for transporting Canadian troops from the Mediterranean theater to Great Britain in advance of the Normandy invasion in 1944?

      a. Operation Gold Coast

      b. Operation Goldfake

      c. Operation Golden Nugget

A. Operation Goldfake.

Q. What was the German code name for plans to invade Norway?

A. Weseruebung (Exercise Weser). The plan for the attack was Case N (for north).

Q. What was the code name for the Allied air raid on Hamburg that produced the infamous fire storms?

A. Operation Gomorrah. (Volume 1, pages 12, 147)

Q. What was the name of the British attack on the French naval fleet at Oran in July 1940?

A. Operation Catapult.

Q. What was Operation Violet?

A. The action by the French Resistance in cutting German communication lines in concert with the Normandy invasion.

Q. What was the name of the Norwegian resistance organization that opposed the Nazis?

A. Milorg. For the most part, Norwegians who were anti-Hitler were known as Jossingers while the pro-Hitler Norwegians were called Quislings. Vidkun Quisling was a Norwegian Nazi who is considered the country's greatest traitor. The use of his name in reference to a group, an individual or an act is understood to indicate treason.

Q. Who described the combination of land, air and sea forces working together in war as "triphibian" strategy?

A. British Prime Minister Winston S. Churchill.

Q. What was the task of the commando team known by the code name Anthropoid?

A. The two-man team of Josef Gabcik and Jan Kubis was sent into Czechoslovakia in 1941 to assassinate SS General Reinhard Heydrich. The mission succeeded. (Volume 1, page 85)

Q. Who was nicknamed Cottonhead?
   a. General Matthew B. Ridgway
   b. Prime Minister Neville Chamberlain
   c. Admiral Chester Nimitz
   d. General Theodore Roosevelt, Jr.

A. Admiral Chester Nimitz.

Q. When the Japanese captured Wake Island they rechristened it Otori Shima. What is the English translation?

A. Bird Island.

Q. What was calvados?

A. The apple brandy from Normandy that was the unofficial drink for victory toasts throughout France on June 6, 1944.

FACT The year 1941 was the Year of the Snake in the Buddhist fortune calendar cycle of twelve years. Though any connection with the evil disposition of the reptile and the ambitions of Japan was not made in the empire, the connection was quickly seized upon by Allied propagandists after December 7, 1941.

Q. What was the German code name for the effort to land spies in the U.S. via submarines?

A. Operation Pastorius.

Q. What was the code name for the U.S. attack on the Japanese Navy at Truk in February 1944?
     a. Operation Pearl
     b. Operation Revenge
     c. Operation Hailstone
     d. Operation Glad

A. Operation Hailstone.

Q. What was Operation Flintlock?

A. The U.S. attack on Kwajalein, the largest atoll in the world (18 miles wide by 78 miles long) in January 1943. (Volume 1, page 79)

Q. Identify the European country where an intelligence operation known as the Alliance of Animals worked against the Germans.

A. France. The individuals in the group used animal code names.

Q. What was the code name of Britain's King George VI?

A. General Lyon.

Q. What did Batter Up and Play Ball mean with regard to Operation Torch in 1942?

A. The former indicated that Allied troops were meeting resistance from the French in North Africa, while the latter ordered the Allies to attack.

Q. What was the German code name for the conquest of Gibraltar?

A. Operation Felix.

Q. What were the troops under General Bernard Law Montgomery in the Africa campaign known as?

A. The Desert Rats, a name they earned before Montgomery took command. In this North African photo, Montgomery, left, and an aide are seen talking to General Ritter von Thoma, commander of the Afrika Korps, shortly after his capture.

U.S. Army Photo

Q. What was the name of the proposed pontoon airfield the British seriously considered building off the coast of France to support the Normandy landings?

A. Lily, which never went beyond the development stage.

Q. Who is known as the man who cut a hole in the Atlantic Wall?

A. British General and tank strategist Sir Percy Hobart. His armor designs, such as the flail tank, were instrumental in establishing Allied beachheads in Normandy in 1944.

Q. In Japanese telephone conversations between Tokyo and Washington in 1941, what were the code words used for President Franklin D. Roosevelt and Secretary of State Cordell Hull?

A. FDR was referred to as Miss Kimiko, while Hull was Miss Fumeko. By introducing these and other code names into a seemingly innocuous telephone call, the Japanese Foreign Ministry was able to get an instant reading from its ambassadors in Washington as to the progress of the peace talks. The United States was Minami in the code, and the Army was Tokugawa.

Q. Who were known as the Plus Four?

A. The term was coined by the wife of Secretary of War Henry L. Stimson and meant to indicate her husband, Secretary of State Cordell Hull, Secretary of the Navy Frank Knox, and Secretary of the Treasury Henry Morgenthau, Jr. The implication was that President Roosevelt and his adviser Harry Hopkins frequently met with these men at the same time. Hence a meeting would involve FDR, Hopkins, Plus Four.

Q. What was the British code name for the torpedo-bombing attack on Italian ships at Taranto?

A. Operation Judgement.

FACT U.S. troops enjoyed free outgoing mail service although all enlisted personnel mail was subject to censorship. Officers, on the other hand, were relied on to observe security restrictions and only spot checks of their mail took place. The quickest way to send or receive a letter was by V-mail, a special form which was microfilmed and reconstituted at the receiving end.

Q. To the Germans it was called *Rudeltaktik*, to the British it was...?
A. *Rudeltaktik*, or "pack tactics," was known to the British as the U-boat wolf packs.

Q. What was the name of the Allied army that was almost totally fabricated to deceive the Germans into thinking the invasion of Europe would come at the Pas de Calais rather than Normandy in 1944?
A. FUSAG — First United States Army Group.

Q. What was STAVKA?
A. The Russian Army High Command.

Q. What was the code word the British used in 1939 to advise intelligence agents that war with Germany was unavoidable?
A. Halberd, which was sent in August 1939.

Q. What was the Gun Club in the U.S. Navy?
A. The unofficial name that proponents of aircraft carriers gave to the proponents of battleships as the primary naval weapon.

Q. Who were the Hiwis?
A. Soviet troops who fought with the Nazis against Stalin's Red Army.

Q. What did the U.S. Marines nickname Mount Suribachi on Iwo Jima?
A. Hotrocks. (Volume 1, pages 3, 27, 60, 85, 125 and 135)

Q. What were known as Hun Sleds by the Dutch?
A. The radio detection vehicles used by the Germans to locate Resistance transmitters.

Q. What did the Allies call the underground radio operation in Luxembourg that furnished misinformation to the Nazis?
A. Operation Annie, which broadcast legitimate German news and information as a means of deceiving German troops when it broadcast misinformation.

Q. What did the term Seabees stand for?
A. Construction battalions, also called CB's. (Volume 1, page 105)

Q. Name the U.S. general that the Japanese called the Beast.

A. Army Air Force General George C. Kenney, the officer who commanded air personnel in the southwest Pacific and creator of the parachute fragmentation bomb.

Q. Who was nicknamed the Major of St.-Lô, France?

A. U.S. Army Major Thomas D. Howie, who was killed in combat there and became a symbol for all other U.S. casualties. (Volume 1, pages 34 and 179)

Q. Who was Swift Heinz?

A. German General Heinz Guderian. The nickname was first applied by his own troops during the German thrust toward the English Channel in 1940.

Q. What was Audie Murphy's nickname?

A. The most decorated U.S. soldier ever by the time he was twenty years old, Audie Murphy was called Baby. (Volume 1, page 105)

Q. Identify the two Allied intelligence personnel known as Big Bill and Little Bill.

A. William Stephenson, who was also known as Intrepid, was the head of British intelligence in New York and was Little Bill. William Donovan, the chief of the American OSS and the first recipient of the four highest U.S. decorations, was known as both Big Bill and Wild Bill. The decorations: Congressional Medal of Honor, Distinguished Service Cross, Distinguished Service Medal and the National Security Medal.

Q. Identify the naval battle that British military theorist Basil Liddell Hart called Strategic Overstretch and became known in postwar Japan as Victory Disease.

A. The Battle of the Coral Sea, because of its boldness and slight chance of success for Japan. (Volume 1, pages 31, 171 and 173)

FACT Much is made of the harsh winter the Germans faced in their Russian campaign in 1941. "General Winter" was considered the Soviet reserve secret weapon. It was the coldest winter in 140 years.

Q. Name the German aircraft nicknamed Iron Annie.
A. The Ju-52 transport.

Q. What did the Morse code message KDHP mean when sent by the U.S. Merchant Marine?
A. It was similar to an SOS in that it indicated the sending ship had been hit by torpedoes.

Q. Identify the U.S. general who used the code name Howe during the North Africa invasion:
      a. George S. Patton
      b. Dwight D. Eisenhower
      c. James M. Gavin
A. General Eisenhower, whose more frequently used code name was Duckpin. (Volume 1, page 13)

Q. What was the GAPSALS?
A. The Give a Pint, Save a Life Society formed by radio personality Arthur Godfrey.

Q. What was the code name of the planned, but not executed, Allied attack on Hitler's headquarters at Berchtesgaden in support of the Allied invasion of Normandy?
A. Operation Hellbound, which was to be carried out by the U.S. Fifteenth Army Air Force based in Italy. It was feared that the Germans would conclude from the attack that the Allies had broken German codes.

Q. What was FIDO?
A. The name for the Allied system of eliminating fog at airstrips in England: Fog Investigation and Dispersal Operation. By using pipes to pump gas that was then ignited and burned off the heavy fog, the Allies managed to keep the airstrips open.

FACT The term Nasos, not Nazis, was the original abbreviation for the National Socialist German Workers' Party. However, German writer Konrad Heiden, who had little use for them, bastardized Nasos into Nazi as a means of poking fun at them. Nazi is derived from a Bavarian word that means "simple-minded."

Q. What was the nickname the leathernecks on Guadalcanal gave to Henderson Field?

A. Bull's Eye, because it was so frequently hit by the Japanese.

Q. What did the word asdic stand for? (Asdic was the British equivalent of sonar.)

A. At the end of World War I, the Royal Navy was assisted in its efforts to combat German U-boats by Allied scientists who were part of the Anti-Submarine Detection Investigation Committee, hence the name asdic.

Q. What was a *Pillenwerfer*?

A. A device created to thwart sonar from Allied anti-submarine vessels. It ejected small gas bubbles that returned an echo similar to a submarine's.

Q. What was Operation Bronx Shipments?

A. The code name for the transfer of material needed for the atomic bomb from the U.S. to Tinian Island in July 1945 aboard the cruiser *Indianapolis*.

Q. What was Huff Duff?

A. The High-Frequency Direction-Finding equipment which the Allies developed to locate German U-boats.

Q. What were Hedgehogs?

A. Anti-submarine cluster weapons consisting of two dozen individual bombs attached to a single projectile. They opened into a spread pattern, thereby increasing greatly the chances of striking a target. The concept was first developed by the Royal Navy at the suggestion of U.S. Navy Captain Paul Hammond.

Q. Identify the two Allied commanders nicknamed Bomber and Tooey.

A. Sir Arthur Harris of the RAF was Bomber and General Carl Spaatz was Tooey. Spaatz (right) joins British Air Chief Marshal Sir Arthur Tedder (left) and Soviet Deputy Commander in Chief Georgi K. Zhukov in a toast at Russian headquarters in Berlin on May 7, 1945, to celebrate the German surrender.

U.S. Army Photo

Q. What was an Anderson Shelter?

A. A simple, cheap and quickly erected structure of concrete and cor-
rugated iron widely used in private gardens throughout Britain to
protect civilians during air raids. It was credited with saving
thousands of lives and was designed by Scottish engineer Sir
William Paterson and inspired by Sir John Anderson.

Q. What was the code name for U.S. troops stationed in Ireland:
     a. Force Green
     b. Shamrock
     c. Magnet

A. Magnet

Q. What was Mackerel the German code name for?

A. Ireland.

Q. What was the Allied code name for Ho Chi Minh, a U.S. ally during the war and adversary in the 1960s?
     a. Lucifer
     b. Lucius
     c. Lulu

A. Ho Chi Minh of Vietnam was known as Lucius.

Q. Who or what were the Maquis?

A. The name identified the French Resistance fighters.

Q. Name the U.S. fighter ace whose plane was named *Marge*.
     a. Pappy Boyington
     b. Richard Bong
     c. Thomas B. McGuire
     d. David McCampbell

A. Richard Bong's P-38 was *Marge*. (Volume 1, page 214)

Q. What nickname did U.S. Marines give to leatherneck fliers?

A. Airedales. The term was popular with the ground support crews.

Q. What was the code name for the U.S. offensive in Burma that had
as its objective securing the Burma Road?

A. Operation Galahad.

Q. What were Kriegies?

A. Allied prisoners of war. The term is a short version of the German word for war captive.

Q. What was the Kreisau Circle?

A. The anti-Hitler movement that wanted to get rid of him by non-violent means. The majority of its members were rounded up and executed after the July 20, 1944, plot to kill Hitler failed.

Q. What was the code name for the British airborne invasion of Sicily?
    a. Ladybird
    b. Ladbroke
    c. Ladbrine

A. Ladbroke.

Q. Which Pacific amphibious invasion was nicknamed Love Day by the U.S. Marines?

A. The April 1, 1945, invasion of Okinawa (Operation Iceberg), because of the moderate to light resistance at first.

Q. What did the British come to call the destruction of secret papers in Cairo on the day it appeared that Rommel would soon overrun the Egyptian capital?

A. Ash Wednesday, because they burned everything and anything they could, rather than chance it falling into German hands.

Q. What was the code name of the RAF plan to raid the prison in Amiens, France, in 1944 in the hope the disruption would result in Allied escapes?

A. Operation Jericho, which succeeded in permitting more than 245 persons to escape. Many of them were facing death sentences from the Gestapo.

Q. What was the Allied code name for the Philippine Islands?
    a. Excalibur
    b. Excelsior
    c. Expedient

A. Excelsior.

The War on Land

Q. Identify the most decorated unit ever in U.S. history.

A. The 442nd Regimental Combat Team, whose motto was "Go for Broke," consisted of Japanese-American volunteers, won 4,667 major medals, awards and citations, including 560 Silver Stars — 28 of which had oak-leaf clusters — 4,000 Bronze Stars, 52 Distinguished Service Crosses and one Medal of Honor, plus 54 other decorations. It also held the distinction of never having a case of desertion. The majority of soldiers in this unit served while their relatives in the U.S. were being held in the infamous detention centers and camps created by the panic after Pearl Harbor.

Q. Name the only two professional sports that were prohibited during the war.

A. Automobile racing, because of its consumption of fuel, and horse racing, which was ruled as nonessential to the war effort.

Q. Who was Winston Churchill's double?

A. Alfred Chenfalls, who was killed in the same plane crash that took the life of actor Leslie Howard. (Volume 1, page 76)

FACT The American flag first flown over Berlin in July 1945 had also flown over the U.S. Capitol in Washington the day the U.S. declared war on Japan, December 8, 1941. (Volume 1, page 2)

Q. Identify the two German divisions that made up the Afrika Korps.

A. The 5th Light (which became the 21st Panzer) and the 15th Panzer. Erwin Rommel was named commander on February 6, 1941, of only these two divisions. Later his command included, in addition to the Afrika Korps, the 90th Light and six Italian divisions. He arrived in Tripoli on February 12, 1941.

Q. Who was Adolf Hitler's favorite actress?
   a. Shirley Temple
   b. Marlene Dietrich
   c. Greta Garbo
   d. Gloria Swanson

A. Der Fuehrer liked Greta Garbo.

Q. Identify the major U.S. city mayor who made propaganda broadcasts to the Italians urging them to dispose of Mussolini and join the Allied cause?

A. Fiorello LaGuardia of New York City, an American veteran of the First World War.

Q. Name the legendary U.S. industrialist whose framed photograph was frequently seen on Adolf Hitler's desk.

A. Automotive pioneer Henry Ford, who also kept a framed photo of the Nazi leader on his desk in Dearborn, Michigan. In *Mein Kampf* Hitler included some anti-Semitic views attributed to Ford.

Q. Name the only major league baseball player who served in both world wars.

A. Hank Gowdy, who was a member of the New York Giants and Boston Braves between 1910 and 1930.

Q. Who designed the camouflage print for U.S. service uniforms?

A. Norvell Gillespie, the garden editor of *Better Homes and Gardens* magazine. (Volume 1, page 83)

FACT German rocket expert Wernher von Braun failed mathematics and physics while attending school at the French Gymnasium. However, he subsequently mastered both subjects in later years.

Q. Who preceded General Hideki Tojo as prime minister of Japan?

A. Prince Konoye, who resigned in October 1941 after President Franklin D. Roosevelt rejected his plea for a summit meeting. Both the prince and Emperor Hirohito were anxious to avert war, while Tojo and the Supreme War Council thought war was the only solution to Japan's problems. In photo above, Tojo is seen in captivity awaiting the Tokyo War Crimes trials.

Exclusive Photo by George Schroth

FACT The Allies tried 199 persons during the International War Crimes trials at Nuremberg. Of these thirty-six received death sentences, five took their own lives while the trials were in progress, twenty-two were sentenced to life in prison, 103 got lesser terms and thirty-eight were acquitted. Crimes against humanity performed in occupied countries accounted for other trials in the specific countries involved for other defendants.

Q. Who wrote the script for the recruitment film *Women in Defense* that was intended to encourage female enlistments?

A. Mrs. Franklin D. Roosevelt. Katharine Hepburn did the narration.

Q. Identify the first member of the U.S. Senate to enlist and face combat in the war.

A. Senator Henry Cabot Lodge II of Massachusetts, who served in North Africa. Representative Lyndon B. Johnson of Texas was the first congressman to enlist. (Volume 1, page 93)

Q. Identify the wartime leader who rejected a German offer of a prisoner exchange that included the return of his own son.

A. Joseph Stalin. His son Jacob eventually died in a German prison camp.

Q. Who produced the Voice of America radio show?
   a. Arthur Godfrey
   b. John Houseman
   c. Edward R. Murrow

A. John Houseman, best known now for his investment commercials on TV and as the star of the TV series *Paper Chase*.

Q. Identify the Republican member of President Franklin D. Roosevelt's Cabinet during the war who had been the GOP vice presidential candidate in 1936 against the Roosevelt ticket.

A. A World War I Army veteran who attained the rank of major (but was constantly called Colonel afterwards for some unknown reason), Secretary of the Navy Frank Knox was one of two prominent Republicans in Democrat Roosevelt's Cabinet. The other was Secretary of War Henry L. Stimson, a former Rough Rider with Teddy Roosevelt.

Q. Identify the avenue in Paris where the Germans marched 250 troops behind a band almost every day during the occupation.

A. The Champs-Elysées, playing military music. The tune most frequently heard was Prussia's Glory. In photo above, U.S. troops follow the same route of march immediately following the City of Light's liberation.

U.S. Army Photo

Q. Name the high-ranking military and political figure that Heinrich Himmler discredited by presenting evidence showing his wife to be a former prostitute.
A. Field Marshal and Reich War Minister Werner von Blomberg. Hitler had been a witness at his wedding only weeks earlier. The scandal forced Blomberg's resignation.

Q. How did Himmler manage to eliminate German Army Chief of Staff General Werner von Fritsch?
A. With fabricated evidence "proving" he was a homosexual.

Q. Name the Nazi whose wife cited thirty women as mistresses when she tried unsuccessfully to divorce him in 1938.
A. Joseph Goebbels. Hitler forbade the divorce.

Q. Identify the wartime boat designer/manufacturer who earned a reputation for building boats for rum runners and bootleggers prior to the war.
A. A. J. Higgins, Jr., whose most touted effort was the Higgins Boat landing craft.

Q. Identify the U.S. Marine Corps Japanese language interpreter who is credited with capturing over half of the prisoners on Saipan in June and July 1944.
A. Guy Gabaldan, whose military exploits were depicted in the movie *Hell to Eternity*. Gabaldan was with the 2nd Marine Division. (Volume 1, pages 105 and 199)

Q. What was the highest German decoration in the war?
A. The Knight's Cross.

FACT Adolf Hitler married his mistress Eva Braun shortly before they allegedly took their own lives. However, no less than five other top-ranking Nazis had mistresses but failed to follow suit. The men, and their women, were:
      Heinrich Himmler and Hedwig Potthast
      Joseph Goebbels and Lida Baarova
      Martin Bormann and Manja Behrens
      Josef Mengele and Irma Griese
      Adolf Eichmann and Maria Masenbucher

FACT The cavalry remained a functioning part of U.S. armed forces throughout the war with the continued operation of cavalry school at Fort Riley, Kansas. However, what is believed to be the last mounted action involved the 26th Cavalry Regiment against the Japanese in January 1942 in the Philippines as U.S. forces retreated to Bataan. During the siege of the fortress cavalry horses were slaughtered for food.

Q. Name the dog who was a USMC mascot and made the amphibious landings on Iwo Jima with the 4th and 5th Marine divisions.

A. George, who was apparently one of several hundred canine mascots U.S. troops took into combat with them. In photo above, two U.S. Army servicemen rest somewhere in the Pacific with a four-legged friend.

Exclusive Photo Courtesy of Mrs. Frank F. Wall

Q. Who was Fritz Kuhn?
A. Chief of the German American Bund.

Q. Name the first Hollywood actor drafted in the war.
  a. Ronald Reagan
  b. Jimmy Stewart
  c. Clark Gable
  d. Sterling Holloway
A. Sterling Holloway.

Q. Identify the eight British air and naval bases transferred to the U.S. by agreement on March 27, 1941.
A. The eight were Antigua, Bahamas, Bermuda, British Guiana, Jamaica, St. Lucia, Newfoundland and Trinidad.

Q. Identify the two French units that fought so bravely that the German victors gave them an honor guard after the battle for Lille, Loos and Haubourdin.
A. The French IV and V Corps. German General Waeger was so impressed that he permitted French General Molinier to retain his staff car. The incident took place after the successful German campaign against Cassel and Monts des Flandres in May 1940.

Q. Identify the only U.S. army that had written orders mentioning Berlin as an objective.
A. The Ninth Army in a document entitled "Letter of Instructions, #20." Commanding Lieutenant General William Simpson was aware that other armies in the Twelfth Army Group (First and Third) had received instructions that did not include the phrase "advance on Berlin." He believed his army had been selected to beat the Russians, and everybody else, there.

Q. Identify the first German army to surrender to U.S. troops.
A. On May 9, 1945, the Fifth Panzer Army under the command of General Gustav von Vaerst surrendered to General Omar Bradley, one day after Germany officially surrendered in the war. (The first German army to surrender in the war was the Sixth Army under Field Marshal von Paulus, which surrendered to the Russians at Stalingrad.)

Q. Why were so many senior German officers absent from their units when the Normandy invasion began?

A. They had been summoned to Rennes in Brittany for war games, which were to include a paratroop assault and sea landings at Normandy. The date of the games was June 6.

FACT The first GI barber shop on the Normandy beaches was operated by Victor Lombardo approximately 1,000 feet from the shoreline on Utah Beach. In photo above, Lombardo, who was with the Quartermaster Corps, tends to the needs of dental technician Sam Kravetz of the 1st Engineer Special Brigade.

Exclusive Photo Courtesy of Murray D. Lombardo

> **FACT** Of the nearly 3 million Allied troops massed in England for the Normandy invasion, 176,475 personnel actually took part in the initial assaults. They brought support equipment including 20,111 vehicles.

Q. Who made the greatest advances on D-Day, the British or Americans?

A. The British. However, they were unable to capture their principal objective, Caen, for more than six weeks.

Q. What was German Army strength in the Cherbourg area of Normandy on D-Day?

A. Approximately 40,000 men.

Q. What were Allied casualties during the twenty-four hours of D-Day?

A. Between 10,000 and 12,000, of which 6,603 were U.S.; 946 Canadians; and the rest British, French and other Allies. The British have never released official figures.

Q. What were German Army Group B casualties in the first month after the Normandy invasion?

A. According to its commander, Rommel, "28 generals, 354 commanders and approximately 250,000 men."

Q. What was the purpose of the 2nd and 5th Rangers' assignment to scale the nearly vertical 100-foot cliffs on Normandy at Pointe du Hoc?

A. Their objective was to knock out six long-range guns capable of hitting either Omaha or Utah Beach. Of the 225 Rangers who participated, 135 were casualties. Ironically the guns had not yet been installed and were still en route.

Q. Which sector of "Bloody Omaha" Beach had the fiercest fighting?

A. Dog Green. Casualties, such as those of Company C of the 2nd Ranger Battalion, which lost fifty-eight of its seventy men, were widespread.

> **FACT** The Allies used a plastic explosive that resembled cow manure in appearance as a road vehicle land mine.

Q. Identify the first U.S. military forces to set foot inside Tokyo.

A. Admiral Lewis Smith Parks, commander of Submarine Squadron Twenty, arrived at Tokyo to participate in the surrender ceremonies and made a secret visit to the Emperor's Palace before General Douglas MacArthur. In photo above, tank 30 of A Company is seen at Sasebo Naval Base. It was the first tank ashore in the amphibious landing of the U.S. 5th Marine Division at Kyushu. Hitching a ride on the tank are members of the infantry of the 26th Regiment, 5th Division.

U.S. Marine Corps Photo

Q. What is the name of the French hamlet in Normandy behind the sand dunes and the beach the Allies code-named Utah?
A. La Madeleine.

Q. Who appeared on Sword Beach on D-Day to welcome the invading British troops?
A. The mayor of Colleville-sur-Orne, replete with a bright brass helmet and proper formal clothes. His village was about one mile inland.

Q. Name the ten U.S. Japanese Relocation Center camps where U.S. citizens were sent following the panic of Pearl Harbor and held throughout the war.
A. The ten camps were Gila River and Poston in Arizona; Manzanar and Tule Lake in California; Granada, Colorado; Topaz, Utah; Heart Mountain, Wyoming; Minidoka, Idaho; and Rohwer and Jerome in Arkansas. (Volume 1, page 73)

Q. Which member of Hitler's inner circle was born in Cairo, Egypt?
A. Rudolf Hess.

Q. Identify the first person executed by the British for treason during the war.
A. George T. Armstrong, a sailor in the Royal Navy who passed on information to the Germans via their consul in New York. Captured by the FBI he was turned over to the British and was hanged on July 9, 1941.

Q. Name the first member of Parliament killed in the war.
A. Ronald Cartland, who died in 1940. He was the brother of romance novelist Barbara Cartland. She, in turn, is related by marriage to Princess Diana, wife of British Crown Prince Charles.

FACT John Amery, son of British Parliament member Leopold Amery, was executed in 1945 for treason after trying to recruit British internees in Germany to fight against the Soviet Union. It was his father's stinging denunciation of Prime Minister Neville Chamberlain that ushered in the collapse of that government. (Volume 1, page 62)

> **FACT** A handful of British advocates of tank and armored warfare prior to war were not taken as seriously as it was later proved they should have been. Captain B. H. Liddell Hart, Colonel J. F. C. Fuller, General Sir Frederick (Tim) Pile and General Sir Percy Hobart were among them. The outspoken Hobart managed to offend his superiors to such a degree that he was actually forced to serve as a corporal in his local Home Guard during a period when his theories were considered unfounded. He is credited with developing flame-throwing tanks, ditch-crossing tanks, pillbox-smashing tanks and others, which his detractors called "funnies." The Germans, however, appreciated and copied many of his ideas.

Q. Where and when was the greatest tank battle in history?

A. At the Kursk salient in the Soviet Union between the Germans and Russians from July 4 to 22, 1943. More than 3,600 tanks were involved.

> **FACT** The cost of an American M-3 tank in 1941 was under $34,000, just about the U.S. price of a Mercedes in 1981. However, by 1981 the price tag on an XMI tank was over $2 million.

U.S. Army Photo

FACT Nazi Germany built two giant tanks called Mammoths that they
tested in June 1944. These vehicles were thirty feet long, weighed
185 tons and had steel plating 9½ inches thick. Unfortunately
they ruined any roads they were driven on, crushing cobblestone
into powder. When they traveled on dirt roads they sank deep
into the earth. Designed by automaker Dr. Ferdinand Porsche,
they were destroyed by the Germans at Kummersdorf in late 1944
so they would not fall into the hands of the advancing Allies.

Q. Name the U.S. Army chaplain that General George S. Patton
ordered to write a prayer for good weather.

A. While Patton was preparing to move units of the Third Army toward
Bastogne to relieve the 101st Airborne during the Battle of the
Bulge in 1944, he ordered Chaplain James H. O'Neill to write a
prayer so the weather would improve and he could make rapid progress. The prayer was written, Patton read it, the weather improved
and the chaplain was given a Bronze Star by the general.

Q. Identify the only two types of tanks that had six-man crews.

A. The U.S. M3 Lee/Grant 31-ton, 18'6" long tanks (4,924 made) and
the German 74.8-ton, 22'3" long Elephant (90 made). The Elephant
had the lowest production of any tank in the war.

Q. What was the strength of a German Leichte Divisionen (light division) as compared to a panzer division?

A. A light division had two motorized rifle regiments and a single tank
battalion for a total of 80 tanks. A panzer division had 324 tanks.
Figures given are tactical strengths in 1940 and may have
changed as the war progressed.

FACT The German panzer divisions' swift victories over the French in
1940 were partially due to the tactical planning and refueling
techniques they employed. French tanks were slowly refueled by
tankers while the Germans accomplished the same results using
handier "jerricans." During the battle for the Meuse, for instance,
the French 1st Armored Division (156 tanks) was virtually wiped
out as it refueled. It was surprised and attacked by the XV Panzer
Corps.

> **FACT** The Soviets had more than four times the number of tanks than the Germans. In all, Russia used more than 21,000 tanks in the war.

Q. What distinction does Nazi Rudolf Hess hold with regard to the Tower of London.

A. He is the last person to have been incarcerated there. (Volume 1, pages 106, 144 and 195)

Q. Identify the first British officer to win a Victoria Cross in the war.

A. Army Captain Harold Ervine-Andrews of the Lancashire Regiment at Dunkirk in 1940.

Q. In which area of combat readiness did France and Germany have the greatest contrast at the outbreak of war in 1939?

A. The French had seven motorized divisions, while the German Army had only four. A fifth, however, was made up of the Waffen (military) SS. In addition, Germany had six panzer (armored) divisions for which the French had nothing comparable. In photo above, a tank that did not survive the liberation of Paris in August 1944 rests on the fringe of the Place de la Concorde.

Author's Collection

> **FACT** General Hideki Tojo resigned as Japanese Premier on July 20, 1944, the same day that the German generals' plot to kill Hitler failed. (Volume 1, pages 55 and 85)

Q. Where were the few remaining survivors who were arrested for the plot to kill Hitler kept?

A. Lehrterstrasse Prison, in Berlin. Approximately 7,000 persons were initially arrested. Just over 5,000 were quickly executed.

Q. After war began in Europe, when was the first attempt made on Hitler's life?

A. Slightly over two months later, November 8, 1939, when a bomb exploded in a Munich beer hall, killing nine people. Hitler had left the area less than a half hour earlier.

Q. Who was the last person to see Adolf Hitler alive?

A. His valet, Heinz Linge.

Q. Identify the two cities selected to be host to the Olympics in 1940 and 1944.

A. After Berlin in 1936, Tokyo was to host the 1940 games while London had been selected for the event in 1944. Neither was held.

Q. Name the two Jews on the German Olympic Team of 1936.

A. Rudi Ball on the soccer squad and Helene Mayer in fencing.

Q. Identify the first U.S. outpost to fall to enemy hands in the war.

A. Guam, where 153 U.S. Marines armed with nothing larger than .30-caliber machine guns tried to hold back a Japanese invasion force of 6,000 troops in early December 1941. It was not recaptured until August 1944.

Q. Who was Hitler's personal secretary?

A. Gertrude Junge.

> **FACT** A plan to assassinate Adolf Hitler by using a telescopic rifle was termed "unsportsmanlike" by the British in 1940. The idea was proffered by Lieutenant General Sir Frank Mason-MacFarlane, who had been a military attaché in Berlin prior to hostilities.

Q. Who was the first U.S. Army paratrooper killed in combat?

A. Private John T. MacKall, who was killed by aerial gunfire while still in the aircraft taking him to the North Africa Theater of Operations. The plane that attacked was French.

Q. Name the first U.S. airborne officer killed in combat.

A. Lieutenant Walter W. Kiser, USMC, on Gavutu Island in August 1942 when the 1st Parachute Battalion landed on the northeast coast. However, the 1st Parachute Battalion invaded via the sea rather than from aircraft, since the island was too far for a controlled air drop.

FACT Mohammed Riza Pahlevi became the Shah of Iran upon the abdication of his father on September 16, 1941. He remained in power until January 16, 1979, when he was asked to leave the country by a newly formed government under Shahpur Bakhtiar. During World War II, Iran proved to be a desired R and R stop for Allied troops. Here a U.S. MP makes the rounds of a brothel in Arak in October 1944.

U.S. Army Photo

> **FACT** The American armed forces were the highest paid in the war. A
> U.S. Army staff sergeant earned as much as a British Army cap-
> tain. A U.S. private serving overseas earned sixty dollars per
> month, roughly three times as much as his British counterpart.
> (Volume 1, page 60)

Q. Identify the first airborne attack using sappers.

A. The German assault on Fort Eben Emael, Belgium, led by Captain
Walter Koch. His engineer troops captured nine installations during the first ten minutes in what was considered the strongest fort
in the world. Koch and the 424 men of his unit used 42 gliders to
execute the stunning assault in May 1940.

Q. Name the Polish division that fought on the side of the Soviets.

A. The Kosciusko Division.

Q. Name the German divisions made up of pro-Nazi Dutch and
Norwegian volunteers.

A. Nederland and Nordland.

Q. Name the Nazi concentration camp commander who was tried and
found guilty by the SS of stealing from the state and then executed.

A. Karl Koch, commander of Buchenwald. He was charged and convicted of diverting personal property of inmates for his own use.

Q. Identify the last U.S. Marine to leave Wake Island in 1941 (he was
also the first to return when it was surrendered).

A. Colonel Walter Bayler, who left aboard a U.S. Navy PBY on
December 21, 1941, and returned in September 1945.

Q. Who was Hitler's interpreter?

A. Dr. Paul Schmidt, who assisted during Hitler's meetings with
Chamberlain, Mussolini, Franco and Japanese Foreign Minister
Yosuke Matsuoka.

Q. Which U.S. unit holds the distinction of being the first ground troops
to see combat in Asia?

A. The 5307th Composite Group, known as Merrill's Marauders.

Q. How many Japanese troops were evacuated from Guadalcanal in February 1942?

A. Approximately 12,000 troops were rescued by destroyers from Cape Esperance at the northwestern end of the island. Efforts to use transport ships proved unsuccessful. Above, the wrecked *Kyusyu Maru* is beached, while at bottom, trio of GI's pause for a photo session near another Japanese transport.

Exclusive Photos by Ben Lebowitz

Q. Identify the German unit that wore enemy uniforms in order to capture objectives at Gennep, Nijmegen and Roermond, in Holland, in 1940.
A. The Brandenburg Detachment, which was specially trained in such tactics. They succeeded in capturing the bridge at Gennep but failed in the other two attempts. As the war progressed, such tactics became much more regular by both the Allies and Axis powers.

Q. Name the only two Latin American nations that had combat troops in action during the war.
A. Brazil and Mexico.

Q. Name the Philippine President who had been his country's most decorated soldier in the war.
A. Ferdinand E. Marcos.

Q. Who headed the Philippine puppet government established by the Japanese in October 1943?
A. Jose Laurel, a wealthy nationalist known for his anti-American sentiments.

Q. Who was the ranking Canadian overseas commander in the war?
A. General Andrew G. McNaughton.

Q. Name the only U.S. corps commander in the war who was a National Guard officer.
A. Major General Raymond S. McLain, who commanded the XIX Corps.

Q. Which country holds the distinction of capturing the greatest number of enemy troops in one place at one time?
A. Germany. It captured more than 500,000 Russian troops at Kiev on September 16, 1941. (Soviet figures claim 527,000 captured while German files indicate over 660,000.

FACT The U.S. Marine Corps strength when the country entered the war in December 1941 was 65,000 officers and enlisted men. It hit its peak strength in August 1945, when the total had risen to 485,113. At full strength the Corps had six divisions and five aircraft wings. In addition, 23,000 women served in the Corps.

Q. Identify the Marine Corps unit that was assigned the task of capturing Mount Suribachi, Iwo Jima, in February 1945.

A. Colonel Harry B. Liversedge's 28th Marines. It was personnel from this unit that raised the American flag, a scene captured so dramatically by Associated Press photographer Joe Rosenthal. The photo won the Pulitzer Prize in journalism for Rosenthal and inspired the U.S. Marine Corps War Memorial by sculptor Felix de Weldon.

Q. Who was General Eisenhower able to reach on his red, green and black telephones from his bedroom in England?

A. The red phone scrambled calls with Washington. On the green phone he reached Winston Churchill. His chief of staff was the voice on the black phone.

Q. Who was the Soviet Union's top propagandist?

A. Ilya Ehrenburg, who is credited with writing the infamous "Kill! Kill!" anti-German copy that was printed and broadcast to Soviet troops. Sign above reflects a similar sentiment by U.S. troops against the Japanese. Scene was on Guadalcanal.

Exclusive Photo by Ben Lebowitz

Q. Where and when was the first stand-up land fight between the U.S. and the Japanese?

A. At Tenaru River on Guadalcanal. It revealed that the Marines were more than able to fight the Japanese on their chosen terrain and beat them.

Q. Identify the Hollywood director who won two Academy Awards for documentaries he made during the war.

A. John Ford, who won Oscars for *December Seventh* and *The Battle of Midway*. (Ford filmed Doolittle's planes as they left the USS *Hornet* for the raid on Tokyo.)

Q. Identify the first U.S. correspondent to land on the Normandy beaches on D-Day, June 6, 1944.

A. Warren H. Kennet, a military writer with the now defunct *Newark News* (New Jersey), had the honor. A 44-year newspaper veteran, Kennet died in March 1982. He also had been the only newsman present when the German 19th and 24th armies surrendered to New Jersey's 44th Infantry during the war.

Q. Identify the U.S. newsman credited with creating the nickname Merrill's Marauders as it applied to the 5307th Composite Group.
     a. Ernie Pyle
     b. Bill Mauldin
     c. Jim Shepley
     d. Edward R. Murrow

A. Jim Shepley of Time-Life, Inc.

Q. How did the premature message of the liberation of Paris come to be broadcast?

A. CBS newsman Charles Collingwood had tape-recorded the story in advance and forwarded it to London for use at the appropriate time. However a mixup resulted in its being broadcast on August 23, 1944, two full days before the actual liberation. It was carried throughout the world.

FACT All eleven starting members of Montana State University's 1940–41 football team were killed in the war.

FACT Iva Ikuko Toguri d'Aquino was an American citizen who was visiting a sick relative in Japan when war broke out. A graduate of UCLA with a degree in zoology, she chose to work in the Japanese Broadcasting Company rather than be assigned to work in a factory. Although she insists she was not Tokyo Rose, she received a ten-year prison term for treason after the war plus a $10,000 fine. President Gerald Ford pardoned her in January 1977. The value of the sultry messages broadcast to U.S. troops in the Pacific by Tokyo Rose has always been questioned, since many servicemen enjoyed the music she played and found her remarks laughable. Iva d'Aquino is seen here in custody, shortly after the war ended, tending to a garden in the prison compound.

Exclusive Photo by George Schroth

Q. Name the *Stars and Stripes* staffer who along with another GI entered Berlin in April 1945, before Germany surrendered.

A. Ernie Leiser, who was accompanied by an Army soldier identified as Mack Morris.

Q. Who was Colonel Blimp?

A. The British cartoon character often used to satirize life in the Empire. He was the product of David Low and appeared in the *Evening Standard*.

Q. Identify the British cartoon character used in World War I that was also employed in World War II.

A. Created by cartoonist Bruce Bairnsfather, "Old Bill" brought the same kind of morale and visual points to British military and civilian personnel as Bill Mauldin's "Willie and Joe" did to U.S. troops.

Q. Who created the cartoon character Sad Sack?

A. George Baker, while on the staff of *Yank* magazine. He had worked for Walt Disney prior to being drafted. His better-known Disney animated films include *Bambi*, *Dumbo* and *Pinocchio*. (Vol I, page 127)

Q. Identify the German newspaper reporter who spied on the Japanese for the Russians, was captured in 1941 and hanged in 1944.

A. Richard Sorge, considered by many to have been the most productive spy up till that time.

Q. Identify the American author who managed to get on a Nazi death list because of his treatment of Adolf Hitler's sex life in the book *Inside Europe*.

A. John Gunther, who outlived Hitler and the Nazis.

Q. What was the name of the 32-page booklet all U.S. servicemen received prior to arriving in Britain?

A. *A Short Guide to Great Britain*, which warned of such social blunders as stealing a British soldier's girl and spending money too freely. It also noted: "The British don't know how to make a good cup of coffee. You don't know how to make a good cup of tea. It is an even swap."

FACT More than 56,000 Japanese died during the 1944 campaign to liberate the Philippines by the Allies. Allied losses were slightly under 3,000. Only 389 Japanese were taken prisoner. In photo above, two huge U.S. Army Alligators move forward toward Japanese positions on Leyte Island. The U.S. Navy LSTs in the picture were manned by Coast Guard personnel.

U.S. Coast Guard Photo

FACT Adolf Hitler became a millionaire as a result of the royalties he earned from his book *Mein Kampf*. The first part of the book was written while he was in Landsberg Prison in 1925, but he added considerably more afterward. Once he came to power, Hitler arranged for copies to be given to newlyweds in the Reich, and it was this widespread distribution that increased his wealth.

Q. Identify the Swedish businessman who spied on the Nazis for the U.S. and was the subject of the book and movie titled *The Counterfeit Traitor*.

A. Eric Erickson, who died in January 1983 at the age of ninety-two. He was so convincing in his role as a pro-Nazi that he lost most of his friends. He was instrumental in passing German synthetic oil secrets on to the Allies. After the war he was honored for his work and invited to meet President Harry S. Truman.

Q. In what city did Anne Frank live when she was caught?

A. Amsterdam, Holland.

Q. Name the city Hitler intended to designate as the new German capital when the war ended.

A. Linz, Austria, his boyhood city.

Q. What was the distance the Afrika Korps was forced to cover in its retreat from El Alamein?

A. Approximately 1,750 miles. It was one of the longest retreats in history.

Q. Where were the majority of German torpedoes manufactured?

A. In the Paris suburb of Saint-Cloud in an underground factory code-named Pilz (mushroom). Though Germany required fewer torpedoes after 1943, Pilz production did not drop off. By the time Paris was liberated, Pilz contained an enormous stockpile of these never-to-be-used weapons.

Q. Who is credited with being the leader of the first organized resistance movement in occupied Europe?

A. General Draza Mihajlovic of Yugoslavia. He not only fought the Nazis, but at times also fought against Tito's partisans.

FACT Martin Bormann, who was sentenced to death in absentia by the Nuremberg War Crimes trials and whose whereabouts are still undetermined, began a program of transporting gold, jewels and art treasures to South America toward the end of 1943. The booty was transported in U-boats, and much of it is thought to have gotten to Argentina, where it was used to finance the later arrivals and provide sanctuary for numerous Nazis who are believed to still be there.

Q. Where did the French officially surrender to the Germans on June 21, 1940?

A. At Compiègne and, by Hitler's request, in the same train car in which the French had accepted Germany's surrender on "the eleventh hour of the eleventh day of the eleventh month" in 1918. In this photo Hitler and other ranking Nazis are seen leaving the train car.

Ullstein Photo

> **FACT** Over 100 Soviet combat photographers lost their lives filming the war. One effort, the total filming of twenty-four hours of the war on June 13, 1943, involved nearly 250 cameramen who recorded the conflict from 140 vantage points and produced an eight-reel film that packed movie houses in the U.S. and Britain as well as Russia. The title: *Day of War.*

Q. Besides Lidice, name the other Czech town that the Nazis destroyed in revenge for the assassination of SS General Reinhard Heydrich.

A. Levzacky. (Volume 1, page 85)

Q. Where were General Eisenhower's headquarters during the preparation of the North Africa invasion?

A. Eisenhower set up headquarters on Gibraltar on November 5, 1942.

Q. What was located in the Collège Moderne et Technique in Reims, France?

A. Supreme Headquarters of the Allied Expeditionary Forces (SHAEF), Eisenhower's actual office.

Q. Name the U.S. general who was headquartered in the Ivory Tower.

A. General Douglas MacArthur, in Port Moresby, Papua.

Q. What building, described as a miniature Versailles, once stood at 73 Wilhelmstrasse in Berlin?

A. The palace that had served as the official residence of German presidents prior to the Third Reich. Hitler's Chancellery was at 77 Wilhelmstrasse.

Q. Which branch of the German military had its headquarters at Shell House in Berlin?

A. The Oberkommando der Kriegsmarine (Navy High Command).

Q. Where was the first Jewish ghetto established in Poland in World War II?

A. In Lodz. Totally enclosed and kept secure by the Nazi SS, it came into being in April 1940.

> **FACT** The largest Japanese spy ring was not in the U.S. but in Mexico, where it kept tabs on the U.S. Atlantic Fleet.

FACT The hands on the clock tower at Hiroshima, Japan, stopped at 8:15 A.M. on August 1, 1945. Coincidentally, five days later at the same time, the first atom bomb ever released over a populated area struck the city. The photo above is one of the earliest taken after U.S. troops entered the city and shows the ruins of the domed Agricultural Exhibition Hall in a rare angle from behind. It remains today as a memorial for the first victims of an atomic attack.

Exclusive Photo by George Schroth

> **FACT** Japan tried to build an atomic bomb during the war and the Nazis agreed to help them. However, the Allied navies were able to prevent shipments of uranium from reaching Japan. Prime Minister Hideki Tojo reportedly ordered Toranosuke Kawashina, a former army colonel, to launch an atom bomb project in January 1943, because Tojo felt the war might be decided by atomic bombs. Germany actually sent two tons of uranium to Japan via U-boat but it was sunk before arriving. The top nuclear physicist on the Japanese project was Hideki Yukawa, who won the Nobel Prize in 1949 for his discoveries about the atom. His nuclear energy research had begun in 1941.

Q. Identify the town in Germany where the Nazis conducted efforts to produce an atomic chain reaction.

A. Haigerloch.

Q. Identify the city in the southern United States that employed illiterates as sanitation men as part of national security during the war.

A. Oak Ridge, Tennessee, where the government conducted atomic research projects. It was believed that if classified information that might escape shredding found its way into the garbage collection, illiterate sanitation employees would be unable to compromise security.

Q. Where was the first German killed in Paris by the underground? When?

A. In the Barbes metro station in 1942. He was shot by a Frenchman, Pierre Fabien.

> **FACT** The same day the French government of Paul Reynaud fell in Paris (June 16, 1940) Frédéric Joliot-Curie, the son-in-law of Madame Curie, watched the British ship *Broompark* sail from France with 410 pounds of heavy water that he had removed from Norway. Joliot-Curie had done experiments in producing an explosion from atomic fission, which required heavy water. During the insurrection in Paris in August 1944, Joliot-Curie contributed sulfuric acid and potassium chlorate for Molotov Cocktails he and others would use against the Germans. His efforts and earlier experiments with atomic fission were considered a vital link in the eventual production of an atomic bomb.

FACT On August 7, 1945, the day after the U.S. dropped the first atom bomb, Stalin summoned five top Soviet physicists and ordered them to catch up with the U.S. in atomic research and development. On July 10 1949, the U.S.S.R. detonated its first atom bomb.

Q. Who was the first non-Chinese general ever to be in command of Chinese troops?

A. General Joseph W. (Vinegar Joe) Stilwell, of the United States. He commanded the Chinese Fifth and Sixth armies in Burma in 1942. Waiting to board an aircraft that will take them to Chungking, China, in this September 1944 photo are Stilwell, Major General Patrick J. Hurley and Major General Daniel I. Sultan.

U.S. Army Photo

FACT General von Senger und Etterlin, the German commander responsible for defending Monte Cassino, was a lay member of the
Benedictines. The monastery was also Benedictine, and the only
area to survive without damage was the crypt where St. Benedict
is buried.

Q. Who had been selected to head the German government by the plotters in the July 20, 1944, failed attempt to kill Adolf Hitler?
   a. Field Marshal Erwin Rommel
   b. Admiral Karl Doenitz
   c. Prince Louis Ferdinand
   d. Admiral Wilhelm Canaris
A. Prince Ferdinand, a co-conspirator in the plot and a high-ranking
employee of Lufthansa, who was the grandson of Kaiser Wilhelm
II. (Volume 1, page 85)

Q. Who was the German general also considered as Hitler's replacement if the July 20, 1944, plot had been successful.
A. General Ludwig Beck, who had served as chief of staff in 1938 and
was openly anti-Nazi.

Q. Name the Israeli general who holds the distinction of being buried
at the U.S. Military Academy at West Point.
A. David (Mickey) Marcus, who was a U.S. Army colonel in World War
II and afterwards became Israel's first general since biblical times.
He was shot by an Israeli soldier in 1948, when he failed to properly identify himself in a restricted area. His life was the subject of
the book and movie *Cast a Giant Shadow*.

Q. Identify the church in Prague where the assassins of SS General
Reinhard Heydrich hid.
A. Karl Borromaeus Church. (Volume 1, page 85)

Q. Identify the first German general to become a casualty after the
Allied invasion of Normandy.
A. Wilhelm Falley, commander of the 91st Infantry Division at Normandy on D-Day, June 6, 1944, was fatally wounded by members
of the 508th Parachute Infantry Regiment.

Q. Identify the U.S. Army lieutenant general who was the first choice
to be commander of American forces in Europe. (Note: Eisenhower
was second choice and got the job when this officer was killed in
a plane crash.)
A. Lieutenant General Frank M. Andrews, who was killed in Iceland
in 1943.

Q. Identify the first U.S. army activated overseas during the war.
A. The Fifth Army under General Mark Clark.

FACT Bernard Law Montgomery was not Britain's first choice to command the Eighth Army in North Africa. Lieutenant General W.
H. E. Gott, who was scheduled to assume command, was killed
on August 8, 1942, and Lieutenant General Montgomery was
picked as a replacement. By the time Montgomery and U.S.
General William K. Harrison, Jr., exchanged pleasantries in
England in April 1944, Montgomery had become a British living legend.

U.S. Army Photo

> **FACT** General Dwight D. Eisenhower's first choice to command the 21st
> Army Group for Operation Overlord, the Normandy invasion,
> was British General Sir Harold Alexander. However, Prime
> Minister Winston S. Churchill had other plans for the able general
> and overruled Ike. Churchill hoped that Alexander, as commander
> of the 15th Army Group in Italy, could take Rome and eventual-
> ly open the way to the Balkans. As a result the 21st Army Group
> command was given to Bernard Law Montgomery.

Q. Identify the general who was relieved of command of U.S. Army
II Corps after the German victory at Kasserine Pass, North Africa.
A. Major General Lloyd R. Fredenhall.

Q. Identify the U.S. Army general who was removed from command
and reappointed to it the same day during the Battle of the Bulge.
A. General Robert Hasbrouck, 7th Armored Division.

Q. Identify the high-ranking Nazi who became an SS general after being dishonorably discharged from the German Navy.
A. Reinhard Heydrich.

Q. Identify the first U.S. Marine Corps officer to attain four-star rank.
A. General Thomas Holcomb, who commanded the Corps from 1936
to 1944.

Q. Identify the only U.S. Marine Corps officer to ever command a field
army.
A. Major General Roy S. Geiger, a naval aviator, who was second in
command to U.S. Army General Simon B. Buckner, Jr., when
Buckner was killed during the battle for Okinawa. Geiger immediately assumed command of the Tenth Army.

Q. When General Mark Clark's Fifth Army captured Rome from the
south it was only the third time the Eternal City had been successful-
ly assaulted from that direction. *Bonus Question:* Name the other
two conquerors and when they did it.
A. In A.D. 536 General Belisarius of the Eastern Empire became the
first, and the feat was not duplicated until 1849, when Giuseppe
Garibaldi took Rome from the south and ended papal rule.

FACT Kaiser Wilhelm II, who led Germany in World War I, despised
Hitler. However, one of his sons, a devout Nazi, became an SS
general. The Kaiser did, nonetheless, send Hitler a congratulatory
wire after the fall of France. He took particular delight in the
reuse of the old train car as the site of the capitulation. Above,
the Kaiser's statue in Koblenz hangs upside down from its
pedestal. The monument was destroyed during the U.S. Third
Army's battle for the city in 1945.

U.S. Army Photo

Q. Why did Hitler replace General Heinz Guderian as Chief of the General Staff in 1945 as the Allies closed in on Berlin?

A. Because of a confrontation between them on March 27, 1945, in which Guderian told Hitler the frank truth about the strength of the German armies expected to defend Berlin. It has been described as a loud, rough exchange that made others present fear Guderian would be arrested for insubordination.

Q. Identify the three British generals who were captured by Rommel's Afrika Korps when their driver got lost in the desert and drove up to an enemy patrol.

A. Generals Richard N. O'Connor, Philip Neame and Carton de Wiart, on April 6, 1941. O'Connor escaped from an Italian POW camp later in the war and commanded the VIII Corps during the Normandy invasion in June 1944.

Q. What distinction do U.S. Army privates C. H. Kuhl and P. G. Bennett hold?

A. They share the dubious honor of having been slapped by General George S. Patton in 1943. Kuhl was slapped on August 3 and Bennett on August 10.

Q. How many hours after General Douglas MacArthur had been notified of the Pearl Harbor raid was Manila attacked?

A. Between eight and nine hours. Yet, as at air bases in Pearl Harbor, his planes remained on the ground and were easy targets.

Q. Identify the Italian and Greek army commanders who faced each other when Italy invaded Greece on October 28, 1940.

A. General Sebastiano Visconti-Prasca, in command of the Ninth and Eleventh Italian armies and General Alexander Papagos who led the Greek forces. The Italians put nearly 88,000 troops against the Greek forces reported to be 150,000 strong.

FACT U.S. General Douglas MacArthur's mother apparently had a difficult time accepting that her child was a boy. Until he was eight years old she kept him dressed in skirts and wearing his hair in long curls.

FACT Of the 4,800 German troops in Colonel Dietrich von Choltitz's command during the battle of Sebastopol, only 347 survived. As a general, von Choltitz was the commander of Greater Paris, which turned out to be his last command. (Volume 1, pages 18, 48 and 126)

Q. Identify the first German officer to land in Holland and the Low Countries when the invasion started on May 10, 1940.

A. Lieutenant Colonel (later general) Dietrich von Choltitz, hero of Sebastopol and the man who disobeyed Hitler's order to destroy Paris. In this August 26, 1944, photo, von Choltitz is being interrogated by U.S. Army Major Sterling H. Abernathy after Paris was liberated.

U.S. Army Photo

Q. Whom did General von Choltitz relieve as commander of Paris?

A. General Hans von Boinseburg-Lengsfeld.

Q. Identify the German military intelligence officer whom the Russians offered a $250,000 reward for.

A. General Reinhard Gehlen, known as the Spy of the Century, who was an expert on the East. When he lost favor with Hitler he escaped to the West and turned over all his files on the Red Army to the U.S. (Volume 1, page 36)

Q. Name the U.S. general most responsible for creating the hysteria and panic that led to the confinement of Japanese-Americans in relocation centers.

A. Lieutenant General John L. DeWitt who told the Secretary of War that the Japanese in the U.S. were preparing sabotage: "The very fact that no sabotage has taken place to date is a disturbing and confirming indication that such action will be taken...the Japanese race is an enemy race...racial strains are undiluted." The subsequent relocation is one of the darkest moments in the history of the democracy.

Q. Who did the initial planning for the Normandy invasion?

A. Lieutenant General Sir Frederick Morgan, Eisenhower's assistant chief of staff.

Q. Who was the British commander on Crete when the Germans invaded in 1941?

A. General Bernard Freyberg, who controlled a garrison of 42,000 British and Greek troops. He was forced to evacuate within two weeks after the German assaults. About 18,000 troops managed to get off the island.

FACT Polish General Maczek's 10th Armored Brigade, which escaped from Poland after the Nazi victory, managed to escape from France after that country began negotiations with the Germans for an armistice. Maczek marched his troops across France and embarked for England. They returned to France with the Allied invasion of Normandy in 1944. In all 24,300 Poles, 5,000 Czechs and 163 Belgian troops made it to England before the armistice.

Q. Identify the French town where General Charles de Gaulle made his first speech after the Normandy invasion.

A. De Gaulle addressed a gathering at Bayeux, France, on June 14, 1944.

Q. Identify the twenty-nine-year-old Free French general in Paris whom de Gaulle charged with gaining control of the Resistance to avoid an unauthorized insurrection?

A. Jacques Chaban-Delmas.

Q. Who was the commander of the Free French Forces of the Interior (FFI) before the liberation of Paris?

A. General Pierre Koenig.

FACT In an effort to repair relations with French General Charles de Gaulle, Supreme Allied Commander Dwight D. Eisenhower designated the 2nd French Armored Division to head the advance toward the liberation of Paris. It was the only French division in Europe. In this photo Major Jacques Massu and chauffeur prepare to enter the outskirts of the city.

Archives Laffont Photo

Q. Name the first SS general to be given command of an army.

A. General Paul Hausser, who had been a lieutenant general in the regular army before joining the SS. He commanded the 7th Army during the Normandy invasion.

Q. Identify the relatively obscure German general whom Hitler put in command of the invasion of Norway.

A. General Nikolaus von Falkenhorst, who, being told his assignment, studied a travel guidebook before presenting a plan of action to Hitler.

Q. Identify the two U.S. generals who actually directed traffic as the troops from Utah Beach began moving inland.

A. Major General Raymond Barton and Brigadier General Theodore Roosevelt, both of the 4th Division.

Q. What became of the American general who at a cocktail party in London in April 1944 carelessly told other officers that the invasion of Europe would take place before June 15?

A. A classmate of Dwight Eisenhower's, he was demoted to colonel, removed from command and sent back to the U.S. He retired.

Q. What was the fate of the British colonel who in April 1944 hinted to civilian friends that the D-Day landings would take place at Normandy.

A. As with the American general who had also been indiscreet, he was demoted and removed from his command. However, he became a member of Parliament after the war.

Q. Name the German general who was considered the third best panzer commander after Guderian and Rommel.

A. General Hasso von Manteuffel.

FACT Contrary to popular belief, James M. Gavin of the 82nd Airborne Division was not the youngest serviceman to become a general in the U.S. Army during the war. Thirty-four-year-old Gerald J. Higgins became a brigadier general in the 101st Airborne. (Volume 1, page 121)

Q. Identify the de Gaulle who arrived in a liberated Paris before the famous general.

A. His son, Philippe, a lieutenant with the 2nd French Armored.

Q. What was Montgomery's objective in the Sicily campaign?
    a. Palermo
    b. Messina
    c. Agrigento

A. Messina, which was taken by Patton, who also took Palermo, Agrigento and, for that matter, most of Sicily.

Q. Who commanded the First French Army, formed after liberation?

A. General Jean de Lattre de Tassigny. One hundred thousand strong, it was part of General Jacob Devers' Sixth Army Group and marched into Germany over some of the most difficult European countryside including the Black Forest and the Vosges. In this picture, some First Army troops in the Mulhouse area of France in November 1944 decorated a jeep with a captured picture of Hitler to which they added their own sentiments.

U.S. Army Photo

FACT U.S. General Omar Bradley, who graduated from West Point in 1915, did not receive his first field command until after the U.S. entered the war in 1941.

Q. Identify the U.S. general who literally lost his pants while being chased by Vichy French police.
   a. George S. Patton
   b. Maxwell B. Taylor
   c. Mark Clark
A. While running from the police after having made a secret visit to North Africa, and removing his pants prior to jumping into a rowboat which was to take him to a waiting submarine, General Mark Clark lost his trousers.

Q. Who replaced the Tojo government in Japan when it fell after the loss of Saipan?
A. General Kuniaki Koiso headed a cabinet that took over the reins of government.

Q. Where did the unauthorized embroidered insignia patches worn by bazooka paratroopers of the 82nd Airborne come from?
A. They were made by nuns in Trapani, Sicily, after the value of bazooka fire gained new respect. James Gavin, commander of the 505th Regimental Combat Team, ordered them.

Q. Identify the only American to hold the rank of field marshal.
A. General of the Army Douglas MacArthur had the rank bestowed upon him by the Philippine, not U.S., government. However, the five-star rank of U.S. services is equal to that of field marshal. (See table of comparative ranks in Appendix.)

Q. Name the German general from whom Hitler took over as Commander-in-Chief of the German army in December 1941.
A. General Walther von Brauchitsch, who had been CIC since 1938. His popularity with Hitler was at its zenith in the early stages of the war with victories in Poland, France and the Low Countries. Once the difficulties of war against Russia became obvious he fell out of favor. However, his early successes earned him a cover on *Time* magazine in 1939.

Q. Who was the one-armed German general that Hitler pulled out of the Stalingrad campaign?

A. General Hans Hube of the Sixth Army.

Q. Identify the location of the first Japanese beachhead in the Philippines campaign in 1941.

A. At Aparri, in the north of Luzon.

Q. Identify the commander of the U.S. Sixth Army for the invasion of Lingayen Gulf, Luzon Island, the Philippines, in 1945.

A. Lieutenant General Walter Krueger, left, shown prior to the invasion with Vice Admiral Thomas Kinkaid, 7th Fleet commander, aboard one of the ships that would carry U.S. troops against the 250,000-man force of Japanese General Yamashita.

U.S. Army Photo

Q. Who was the Japanese defender of the Philippine archipelago?
A. Field Marshal Hisaichi Terauchi.

Q. Who succeeded Marshal Pietro Badoglio as Italian Army Chief of Staff?
A. Ugo Cavallero. Badoglio resigned as a result of the military failures the Italians suffered in Greece. Cavallero replaced him on December 6, 1940.

Q. What was the highest military award in the Soviet Union?
A. Hero of the Soviet Union.

Q. What rank did gold epaulettes with a one-inch-across star indicate on Russian Army uniforms?
A. Field marshal.

Q. Name the three German field marshals who commanded the trio of army groups that invaded Russia on June 22, 1941.
A. Wilhelm von Leeb, Army Group North; Fedor von Bock, Army Group Center; Gerd von Rundstedt, Army Group South.

Q. Identify the first and last men to be named field marshals by Hitler.
A. Werner von Blomberg was the first in 1936, and Ritter von Greim was the last in 1945. In all, Hitler promoted twenty-five generals to field marshal.

Q. Who was the youngest field marshal in German military history?
A. Erwin Rommel, age 50. Hitler elevated him to the position after his stunning successes in North Africa against the British.

Q. Identify the soldier to whom Hitler gave a three-pound gold baton eighteen inches long.
A. Rommel in 1942. However the field marshal never was seen publicly with it after that.

FACT Axis prisoners of war were, for the most part, treated in accordance with the provisions of the Geneva Convention in British and U.S. prison camps. However, prisoners of war in Russian camps experienced an 85 percent mortality rate.

Q. Name the SS general in Rome whom Adolf Hitler ordered to kidnap Pope Pius XII.

A. General Karl Wolff, the playboy SS chief in Italy. Hitler summoned Wolff to Rastenburg on September 12, 1944, two days after the German occupation of Rome, and told him to "...occupy Vatican City...and take the Pope and the Curia to the North. I do not want him to fall into the hands of the Allies."

FACT After the war, German courts found twenty-five SS and Army generals guilty of war crimes and executed them. The Allied powers sentenced another fifty-seven to death. An astonishing total of 101 committed suicide during the war. As a result of combat deaths, accidents, natural causes and the above-mentioned war-crimes convictions and suicides, Germany lost 901 men who had been general officers during the war years. Above, a Nazi Volkssturm (People's Army) general lies on the floor of the Leipzig City Hall after taking his own life rather than surrendering to the U.S. First Army on April 19, 1945. The scene is eighty miles southwest of Berlin.

Ullstein Photo

Q. How many generals did the U.S. have compared to the Germans?
A. Germany had a total of 3,363 generals during the war while the U.S. had just over 1,500.

Q. Identify the Hungarian dictator whose son was kidnapped by Otto Skorzeny to guarantee Hungary's support of Nazi goals.
A. Admiral Miklos Horthy. (Volume 1, page 80)

Q. Name the two European leaders Hitler earmarked for kidnapping after the successful commando raid in Italy that resulted in the rescue of Mussolini.
A. Pétain of France and Tito of Yugoslavia.

Q. Identify the geographic area that was scheduled along with the Marshall Islands to be the target of the first U.S. offensive against Japan in February 1942.
A. Wake Island. However, lacking aircraft carrier support from the USS *Lexington* (CV-2) because of a refueling problem, the attack was only carried out on the Marshalls.

Q. Who was the Gestapo chief in France in August 1944?
A. Karl Oberg.

Q. Identify the first U.S. serviceman to land from a troopship in Great Britain after the U.S. entered the war.
A. Private First Class Melburn Hencke, on January 26, 1942.

Q. Identify the first U.S. soldier to set foot on French soil once the U.S. got into the war.
A. U.S. Army Corporal Frank M. Koons, who was an American Ranger in the Dieppe, France, raid. The first U.S. soldier to land in France during the Normandy invasion, June 6, 1944, was a member of the 101st Airborne Division Pathfinders, Frank L. Lillyman.

FACT Technical Sergeant Milton Shenton of the U.S. Army's 4th Division had the distinction of being point man for the division when it broke across Utah Beach on D-Day and again when they were part of the forces that liberated Paris.

Q. Identify the American singer voted the most popular by troops during the war.

     a. Bing Crosby
     b. Frank Sinatra (shown above)
     c. Kate Smith
     d. Roy Acuff

A. Country-Western singer Roy Acuff.

Exclusive Photo by Joseph De Caro

> **FACT** The United States is the greatest haven for Nazi war criminals, according to estimates of various organizations that continue to hunt such people. In the first thirty-six years following the end of World War II, the U.S. managed to deport only one accused Nazi while it is estimated that upwards of 3,000 others are still living in the country.

Q. Identify the wartime European monarch who fled the Nazis, joined the RAF, eventually worked in public relations in New York, and is the only European monarch buried in the U.S.

A. King Peter II of Yugoslavia who fled ten days after being crowned king in 1941, when the Nazis invaded his country. The British backed Tito as the leader of postwar Yugoslavia, and Peter thus became a king without a country. He died in Denver, Colorado, on November 4, 1970, and is buried in Libertyville, Illinois.

Q. When was Ethiopian Emperor Haile Selassie returned to his country's throne?

A. On May 5, 1941, exactly five years after the Italians had conquered Addis Ababa, the capital.

Q. Where did the Italian royal family re-establish itself after it fled from Rome in September of 1943?

A. Brindisi, far south of Rome. They feared capture by the Germans whom they had just deserted as allies.

Q. Name the song the U.S. 28th Infantry Division marched to on the Champs-Elysées in Paris when they were requested to march in a liberation parade before resuming their advance.

A. "Khaki Bill."

> **FACT** Less than 10 percent of the people considered war criminals for their part in the Nazi extermination camps have ever been brought to justice. According to the West German government, it took approximately 25,000 people to operate the camps. A small portion of them reached freedom through ODESSA, the secret escape organization for former SS members. However, the vast majority of war criminals passed themselves off as refugees at displaced persons camps when the war ended, thereby gaining freedom.

Q. Identify the first U.S. soldier to cross the Ludendorff Bridge at Remagen and set foot on German soil.

A. Sergeant Alexander A. Drabik, a butcher from Holland, Ohio, led a platoon through a barrage of artillery fire at 4 P.M. on March 7, 1945. He was a member of the 9th Armored Division, First Army. In photo above, Private Leroy Johnson of Lakewood, New York, operates a traffic control telephone to direct traffic across the treadway pontoon bridge from Remagen to Erpel, Germany, on March 17, the same day the Ludendorff bridge crumbled. (Volume 1, page 77)

U.S. Army Photo

FACT In an extraordinary move, unequaled in world history, Britain suggested a union with France that would create a new country out of what had been two. The blueprint for the merger was outlined in the Declaration of Franco-British Union, which General Charles de Gaulle read over a phone from London to French Premier Paul Reynaud. De Gaulle and other Frenchmen worked it out with British leaders in the hope that such a union would bolster the morale of the French and make it impossible for France to negotiate a separate armistice or peace with Germany as long as the British Isles remained free. It never came to pass.

Q. Identify the British diplomat, and future prime minister, who was heavily involved in the Allied plan to capture Rome by using airborne troops.

A. Harold Macmillan. Eisenhower had also given approval for Macmillan to be involved in the actual operation, but it never came to pass.

Q. Who was Lieutenant Colonel Hellmuth Meyer?

A. The senior officer in charge of Germany's counterintelligence staff on the European invasion front prior to and during D-Day. The staff was able to intercept calls by military police jeeps over one hundred miles away in England.

Q. Who was the first public official named by de Gaulle in Paris, even before liberation?

A. Charles Luizet, appointed to replace Prefect of Police Amédée Bussière. Luizet had parachuted into France on August 12. He assumed his job on August 19.

FACT When U.S. troops occupied Sicily they learned that there was a serious interest among some Sicilians in having the island become the forty-ninth state in the U.S. By 1947 the effort had come to the point that a Sicilian bandit named Salvatore Giuliano wrote to President Harry S. Truman and asked for help in liberating Sicily. The movement attracted many nationalists who resented Rome's treatment and also sought protection from what they considered a communist takeover of Italy. The separatist cause became a thing of the past by the 1950s as various leaders were unable to unify and settle differences among themselves.

Q. What location became known as the Argonne of World War II?
A. The Hurtgen Forest near Aachen, Germany, because of the heavy casualties sustained during the campaign. Aachen was the first German city captured by American troops. In the photo above, soldiers of the 2nd Battalion, 26th Infantry, are seen involved in street-by-street fighting in Aachen.

U.S. Army Photo

FACT During the invasion of the Low Countries (May 10, 1940) the German commander of the 22nd Infantry Division, General Graf von Sponeck, was so convinced that he would receive a request for an audience from Dutch Queen Wilhelmina that he set out on the campaign in full-dress uniform. His objective was The Hague and also the submission and cooperation of the Dutch Crown. Sponeck did not get his meeting with the queen but instead was wounded in the fierce battle.

Q. Who followed French Premier Daladier as leader of France when he resigned?

A. Paul Reynaud, who proved to be no better than Daladier in coping with the German war machine. (Reynaud was replaced by Henri Pétain, Marshal of France, hero of Verdun in the First World War, on May 17, 1940.)

Q. Who was Germany's ambassador to France at the time of the liberation of Paris?

A. Otto Abetz.

Q. From where did Vichy French Prime Minister Pierre Laval depart from Paris? How? When?

A. From the Hôtel de Matignon, residence of the country's prime ministers on August 17, 1944. The Germans provided an SS-chauffeured car (a Hotchkiss) to take him to Germany.

Q. Identify the first member of the Vichy French government to be tried and found guilty of collaboration.

A. Former Minister of the Interior Pierre Pucheau, who was tried by a military court in Algiers in 1944 and sentenced to death.

Q. Where was Leon Trotsky killed and how?

A. The Russian revolutionary, who, along with Lenin and Stalin, was an architect of communism in 1917, was killed by a Spanish communist in Mexico City on August 21, 1940.

FACT Neville Chamberlain, whose handling of the early war effort and prewar negotiations led to his resignation, died on November 10, 1940, exactly six months after he was succeeded by Winston Churchill as Prime Minister. (Volume 1, pages 62, 66 and 196)

FACT Gasoline, which played such an important role in halting the German advance during the Battle of the Bulge and was at times considered as precious as water to the Allied and Axis tanks in North Africa, was needed in tremendous quantities. An armored division needed more than eight times as much gasoline as it did food and even an infantry division needed six times more gasoline than food. Convoy above is somewhere in France after D-Day.

U.S. Signal Corps Photo

> **FACT** What is regarded as the highest bounty ever put on a human being, the sum of $1 million, was offered for the capture of Adolf Hitler by U.S. industrialist Samuel H. Church in 1940. The conditions were that Hitler be alive and unharmed and that he be tried by an international court set up by the League of Nations.

Q. When did Italy sign the armistice with the Allies?
A. September 8, 1943.

Q. How many of Berlin's 248 bridges did the Germans destroy to slow down the Russian advance on the city in April 1945?
A. Approximately 120 were destroyed.

Q. Which of the Resistance groups in France had the most military and political power?
A. The FTP (Francs-Tireurs et Partisans), which was communist.

Q. Identify the three Frenchmen executed for sabotage at the Farman aircraft works at Boulogne-Billancourt in 1940.
A. Roger and Marcel Rambaud and Maurice Lebeau, all suspected communists. They were charged with weakening locking nuts on fuel nozzles, which caused aircraft to explode in flight.

Q. Identify the European leader who was put on trial for his negligence in not preparing his country for war.
A. French Prime Minister Edouard Daladier, who at the time of his arrest had just resigned as War Minister. He had been Prime Minister when war was declared.

Q. Why were no bronze cents issued by the U.S. government in 1943?
A. The copper was needed for the war effort. Zinc-coated steel cents were issued in that year. However, a few bronze planchets were struck by error and are very rare. Likewise zinc-steel planchets that were struck in 1944 are also rare.

> **FACT** Adolf Hitler received his Iron Cross in the First World War from a Jew, Lieutenant Hugo Gutman.

Q. What was Dwight D. Eisenhower's rank when he arrived in England in 1942?

A. He was a lieutenant general, relatively unknown, who had been put in charge of the invasion of North Africa, Operation Torch, by U.S. Army Chief of Staff General George C. Marshall, In this June 14, 1944, photo at Normandy, France, Supreme Allied Commander Eisenhower and Marshall leave an amphibious vehicle while the Air Force's Commanding General, Henry H. (Hap) Arnold, steps down.

U.S. Army Photo

> **FACT** The United States Marine Corps is almost always thought of with
> regard to the campaigns in the Pacific. However, Marines were
> also involved in the war in Europe with individuals assigned to
> special missions with underground units and Resistance fighters.
> On August 29, 1944, Marines from two U.S. cruisers landed on
> a trio of islands near Marseilles, France, and captured German
> installations. Marines also served on U.S. Navy staffs and as sea-
> going troops on ships during the landings in North Africa, Ita-
> ly, Southern France and Normandy.

Q. Identify the two German coins that were virtually melted out of
existence because of a need for bronze and copper in airplane engine
production.

A. One- and two-pfennig copper coins, which were almost totally nonex-
istent by March 1942. At that time Germany began calling in church
bells to satisfy the production need.

Q. How much silver is in U.S. five-cent pieces minted between 1942
and 1945 and why?

A. Nickel, a critical war material, had been used in U.S. five-cent pieces
since 1866. To indicate a change of alloy in 1942–45, a large "P"
was placed above the dome of Monticello on the reverse of the coin.
Its composition is 35 percent silver, 56 percent copper and 9 percent manganese. In 1946 the old alloy of nickel and copper was again
used.

Q. Identify the only East European leader of a government in exile
whom the Soviets permitted to return home after the war.

A. Eduard Benes of Czechoslovakia.

> **FACT** The famous U.S. Marine Corps raid on Makin Island by Carlson's
> Raiders in 1942 actually worked against U.S. efforts in the Pacific
> despite its much-publicized success. The leathernecks were
> credited with destroying a Japanese base and killing approximate-
> ly 350 enemy troops while sustaining less than forty fatalities.
> However, this bold move by the U.S. prompted the Japanese to
> strengthen other islands that had previously been lightly fortified.
> The result was a higher cost in American lives in campaigns that
> followed.

Q. What did the Germans tell the Sicilians and the Italian Army about
U.S. paratroopers that made those U.S. troops so feared prior to the
invasion?

A. That their units were hardened American murderers and convicts who
were pardoned in exchange for fighting. The widespread practice of
paratroopers shaving their heads did much to substantiate the fears
when Sicilians encountered them. In wartime photo above, note that
rank insignia of first paratrooper has been retouched out.

Imperial War Museum Photo

> **FACT** Before Nazi Germany decided upon its final solution to rid itself of Jews, it had considered sending them to the island of Madagascar, where they would serve as hostages in the event the U.S. threatened to enter the war. However, transportation and logistic considerations were used as an excuse not to carry out the deportation.

Q. What use did the U.S. government find for cartridge cases between 1944 and 1946?

A. They were recycled as pennies. The color of pennies minted was slightly different on new, uncirculated coins but otherwise they were the same. The U.S. resumed using the original alloy of 1864–1942 in 1947.

Q. How many people did the Nazis transport from Paris to Germany on the last train from the French capital to the concentration camps at Ravensbruck and Buchenwald?

A. Approximately 2,450 on August 18, 1944, less than seven days before the first Allied troops entered Paris. Less than 300 of those moved survived the war.

Q. When did Hitler arrive at his bunker under the Reich Chancellery in Berlin for the last time?

A. On January 16, 1945, Hitler came to the Chancellery and remained there throughout the rest of his life.

Q. Who was Alain Perpezat?

A. The young Frenchman who had the unhappy task of delivering the message to the Resistance advising them that the Allies did not intend to liberate Paris but instead would bypass it and continue advancing on retreating German forces. Perpezat did not know the contents of the coded message, which was later reversed.

> **FACT** Major Cyril Barclay of the British Expeditionary Forces purchased several Michelin road maps in France to assist moving his troops to Dunkirk for the evacuation. He had been unsuccessful in obtaining regulation maps from the Army. However, he was refused compensation for the expenditure inasmuch as the Army had no provisions for the retail purchase of maps.

Q. Identify the objective in North Africa that marked the first British offensive there.

A. Sidi Barrani, where General Sir Richard O'Connor's 31,000-man Western Desert Force routed the 80,000-man Italian Army by a surprise rear attack. Over 2,000 Italians were captured in the early hours of the campaign. This photo shows Australian troops in Bren carriers moving across the North African desert.

Imperial War Museum Photo

> **FACT** The Red Cross once owned and operated a company that manufactured arms. During World War II the firm of Oy Sako Ab made over 270 million cartridges for Finland's armed forces. When Soviet troops moved to take over all munitions plants in territories it occupied, the Finns gave the firm to the Red Cross. It remained under their control and manufactured arms, until 1962, when it changed hands again.

Q. Name the site of Rommel's first offensive against the British in North Africa.

A. The March 24, 1941, attack by the 5th Light Division against El Agheila in Libya.

Q. When did the British and Germans first meet in combat in North Africa?

A. February 27, 1941.

Q. Identify the Polish Brigade that along with British troops relieved the Australians at Tobruk in October 1941.

A. The Polish Carpathian Brigade.

Q. Name the three countries that were represented by troops in every theater of the war.

A. All were Allies: The United States, Great Britain and New Zealand.

Q. Identify the first Canadian woman at sea during the war.

A. Fern Blodgett, who earned the distinction in June 1941, when she became a radio operator on the Norwegian cargo ship *Mosdale*.

Q. When did the U.S. announce its neutrality in the European war?

A. September 5, 1939.

> **FACT** Canada did not send draftees overseas until January 1945. There was strong objection to the draft in Canada, and as a result more than 10 percent of the 60,000 draftees were AWOL when the ships departed from Halifax. However, 13,000 Canadian draftees served in the European theater. Prior to their country's entry into the war, Canadian volunteers served with distinction in the RAF and Royal Navy.

FACT The first entire division to receive a Presidential Unit Citation was the 101st Airborne. The photo above was taken during the official presentation and review on March 15, 1945, in France. In the rear of the jeep are General Dwight D. Eisenhower, Supreme Allied Commander, and General Maxwell D. Taylor, commanding general. Deputy Division Commander Brigadier General G. J. Higgins is in front. Driver is unidentified. (Author's note: Photo negative was "flopped" during official processing. As a result steering wheel is on wrong side and jeep ident numbers are backwards!)

U.S. Army Photo

> **FACT** During the British drive to Benghazi they captured over 130,000 Italian troops in North Africa.

Q. How did Austrian-born Adolf Hitler become a German citizen?
A. Wilhelm Frick, while Premier of Thuringia, did the honors by making Hitler a German citizen. Frick went on to become the Nazi Minister of the Interior, Protector of Bohemia and Moravia.

Q. Name the future Pope who passed on intelligence to the American OSS while he was a monsignor in the Vatican.
A. Pope Paul VI, Monsignor Giovanni Montini.

Q. Name the French priest who headed up a Resistance group that manufactured passports, identity cards and other documents in his Marseilles monastery.
A. Father Benoit-Marie de Bourg d'Ire of the Capuchin order. The false documents were used to help Jews, both French and foreign, escape capture by the Nazis and Vichy government. When Italy defected to the Allies and the Germans swept into the Italian-occupied zone of France, Father Benoit moved his operation to Rome.

Q. Who was Monsignor Hugh O'Flaherty?
A. The Vatican cleric who organized an underground network of safe houses and escape routes for Allied prisoners of war who had escaped from the Germans.

Q. Who was Winston Churchill's doctor?
A. Charles Moran.

Q. Who was Adolf Hitler's doctor?
A. Theodor Morell.

Q. Identify the site of the first Allied land victory in the war.
A. Narvik, Norway, on May 28, 1940, when the French Foreign Legion captured the port from the Germans.

> **FACT** New Zealand provided a higher proportion of its population (under 3 million) for war service than any other dominion.

Q. Identify the city that received the greatest number of German V-1
and V-2 bombings.
   a. Coventry
   b. London
   c. Antwerp
   d. Southampton
A. Antwerp, Belgium, which was hit over 3,700 times. London was hit
a total of 2,936 times. (Volume 1, pages 27, 151, 153 and 160)

Exclusive Photo by Joseph Niechwiadowicz

The Air War

Q. Identify the 1636 Olympic Gold Medal winner who participated in the Battle of Britain as a wing commander.

A. Major Gotthardt Handrick, who was a wing commander in the Luftwaffe, not the RAF. He won top Olympic honors in the Pentathlon.

Q. Identify the first U.S. pilot to become an ace in two wars.

A. Although some historians consider the Spanish Civil War as a part of or related to World War II, it was in fact a totally separate conflict. A. J. Baumler, an American veteran of the Spanish war, scored eight kills during action in the CBI Theater.

Q. Identify the first U.S. pilot to equal Captain Eddie Rickenbacker's World War I mark by scoring twenty-six "kills."

A. USMC fighter ace Joe Foss, who also won the Medal of Honor for action over Guadalcanal.

Q. Identify the U.S. Army Air Force general who began his service career as an enlisted man and is credited with shooting down Hermann Goering in World War I.

A. General George C. Kenney.

Q. What was the Japanese Army version of kamikaze called?

A. Tokko tai. Kamikaze indicated Japanese Navy suicide planes only.

Q. .When was Buckingham Palace bombed?

A. On September 13, 1940. The plane that did it was subsequently shot down by RAF Sergeant-Pilot Ginger Lacey of the 501st Squadron. Commissioned later in the war, Lacey became an ace more than five times over, with twenty-eight "kills."

Q. What was the original name for the U.S. P-51 Mustang fighter?
     a. Colt
     b. Apache
     c. Thunderbird
     d. War Horse

A. It was Apache.

Q. Identify the U.S. pilot credited with shooting down Japanese Admiral Isoroku Yamamoto.

A. Captain Thomas G. Lanphier.

Q. Identify the Japanese air ace credited with shooting down Captain Colin P. Kelly, Jr., America's first publicized hero.

A. Saburo Sakai, who is credited with a total of sixty-four "kills" and ranks as Japan's third-highest-scoring ace. (Volume 1, page 214)

Q. Who was the most successful jet pilot ace of the war?

A. Lieutenant Colonel Heinz Bar. Ranked ninth overall among Germany's air aces, Bar scored sixteen "kills" flying the Me-262. His combined total was 220 "kills." Remarkably, he survived being shot down himself eighteen times.

Q. Identify the pilot who flew more than 2,530 sorties and is credited with destroying over 500 enemy tanks.

A. Luftwaffe fighter ace Hans Ulrich Rudel. His total of sorties is the record in the war.

Q. What was the nickname of the U.S.-built Grumman F6F aircraft?

A. The Hellcat, which only saw service in the Pacific Theater. Closeup photo at left is of a Hellcat from the aircraft carrier USS *Saratoga* (CV-3).

Exclusive Photo by Tom Christie

Q. In service slang what did SNAFU stand for?

A. Situation Normal, All Fouled Up. Military personnel were known, however, to substitute a different term for the next to last word. Photo above shows the fuselage of a USAAF bomber at Fenton Field, Australia, with appropriate artwork and the name *SNAFU II*. Kindred slang included: FUBAR (Fouled Up Beyond All Recognition), FUMTU (Fouled Up More Than Usual) and JANFU (Joint Army-Navy Foul Up).

Exclusive Photo by Harold D. Zahler

Q. Identify the high-scoring U.S. air ace who was shot down by Japan's second-highest-scoring ace in action over Los Negros in the Philippines in January 1945.

A. Thomas B. McGuire, Jr., whose score of thirty-eight "kills" was surpassed only by Richard Bong (forty). McGuire was shot down and killed by Shoichi Sugita, Japan's second-ranked ace with eighty "kills." (See footnote on controversial scores for Sugita and Hiroyishi Nishizawa, Volume 1, page 214.)

Q. Identify the Japanese pilot credited with shooting down "Pappy" Boyington.

A. Gregory Boyington, the colorful USMC pilot who was the fifth-ranked U.S. ace in the war (twenty-eight "kills"), was shot down by Masajiro Kawato on January 3, 1944. (Volume 1, page 215)

Q. Name the U.S. serviceman who became the first member of the Army Air Force to bomb Berlin, Rome and Tokyo.

A. Sergeant Kurt Hermann who served with both the Twelfth and Eighth Air forces in Europe. In the Pacific he was assigned to B-29s that bombed Tokyo. He flew more than 105 missions before being reported missing in action in the Pacific.

Q. Identify the future U.S. Vice President who was shot down as a U.S. Navy pilot over Iwo Jima and rescued by submarine.

A. George Bush. The sub that saved him was the USS *Finback*.

FACT The Luftwaffe organized and operated what is considered one of the most successful Trojan Horse operations in the history of warfare with the formation of Kampfgeschwader 200 (KG-200). This extremely secret group penetrated Allied air space by using captured U.S., British and Russian aircraft, complete with flight crews that spoke the appropriate language, dressed in enemy uniforms and passed as Allied fliers. They were used for depositing spies on foreign soil, photo recon and for attacking Allied units that they attached themselves to, usually on return legs from bombing missions over Europe. There were no less than forty-eight KG-200 bases operating out of eleven countries and flying almost everything in the Allied arsenal including B-17s, B-24s, P-51s, Spitfires and Mosquitoes.

Q. What was the Allied code name for Guadalcanal?
A. Cactus, and the pilots who used Henderson Field were called the Cactus Air Force. In this photo, a Japanese Betty bomber rests amid the skeletons of palm trees after it crash-landed. (Volume 1, page 40)

Exclusive Photo by Ben Lebowitz

Q. Identify the Japanese fighter that was modified and produced as a kamikaze toward the end of the war.
A. The Mitsubishi Zero-Sen, known to the Allies as the Zeke. Only 465 Zekes out of nearly 10,450 produced ever became kamikazes. The one in photo above is seen in the water off Guadalcanal.

Exclusive Photo by Ben Lebowitz

Q. Identify the first U.S. armed forces airman to shoot down a German plane.

A. Lieutenant Samuel F. Junkin, USAAF, during the raid on Dieppe, France, August 19, 1942.

Q. Identify the pilot of the first B-17 lost in combat.

A. U.S. Army Air Force Captain Colin P. Kelly, Jr., on December 10, 1941.

Q. Identify the first U.S. pilot to make use of the airfield on Iwo Jima in 1945.

A. Captain Raymond Malo, on March 4, 1945, in a B-29 named *Dinah Might*, was the first of approximately 2,400 emergency landings by U.S. aircrews on Iwo Jima. (Volume 1, pages 3, 27, 60, 85, 125 and 135)

Q. Identify the only member of the RAF to be awarded a Victoria Cross in 1940 for air battle over Britain.

A. Fighter pilot Lieutenant James B. Nicholson. He received it posthumously for attacking a German squadron while his own plane was on fire.

Q. Who was the first fighter pilot to score over 100 "kills"?

A. Lieutenant Colonel Werner Molders of the Luftwaffe. He was also the first pilot to be decorated with the Knight's Cross with oak leaves, swords, and diamonds — Germany's highest award. He was killed in a crash while a passenger in a plane in November 1941, en route to funeral services for General Ernst Udet. By the end of the war thirty-eight German fighter aces scored 100 or more "kills," something no other country in the war was able to do.

Q. What was unusual about the U.S. 99th Fighter Squadron?

A. It was the first Army Air Force unit made up totally of blacks.

FACT The dreaded German fighter Me-109 (Messerschmitt) used American-made propellers and British-made wing slats early in the war.

FACT The largest planned crash landing by the USAAF during the war took place on July 15, 1942, when two B-17s and six P-38Fs were forced down on Greenland because of fake German weather reports which caused them to run low on fuel. The planes had been on their way to Great Britain from Maine, but the crews spent the next ten days on the ice cap before being rescued just forty-five miles from the Arctic Circle. Still there, and believed to be under thirty-five to forty feet of snow, the six P-38Fs are the goal of an extraordinary recovery expedition sponsored by the R. J. Reynolds Tobacco Company. No effort will be made to recover the B-17s. If successful, the team will have more than doubled the number of P-38s left in the world. Of the 9,600 made, only five survived. In photo above, Lieutenant Robert H. Wilson relaxes on his P-38F Lightning. One landed with gear down and promptly flipped. The other five skidded down with gear up, preventing eventual takeoffs. The photo was taken by J. Brad McManus, the first to land.

Photo by J. Brad McManus

Q. Identify the U.S. pilot who shot down four Japanese planes on December 7, 1941.

A. George Welch, who was the first member of the U.S. armed forces to score four "kills" in a single day.

Q. Name the only person to ever become a triple ace in one day by scoring fifteen "kills."

A. Major Wilhelm Batz of the Luftwaffe against the Russians in 1942. He was ranked sixth overall among German aces with 237 "kills."

Q. What was the greatest number of enemy planes ever shot down in a single day by a U.S. pilot and name him?

A. Nine Japanese planes were shot down on October 24, 1944, by U.S. Navy pilot David McCampbell.

Q. Name the first American pilot to become an ace by scoring five "kills" in one day.

A. On December 25, 1941, Robert Hedman, a volunteer pilot with the Flying Tigers, accomplished the feat. However, the first U.S. armed forces pilot to score five "kills" in one day was Lieutenant Edward (Butch) O'Hare on February 20, 1942. Chicago's O'Hare International Airport was named in his honor. (Volume 1, page 138)

Q. Identify the only American killed in the war who is buried in St. Paul's Cathedral in London.

A. William M. Fiske III, who was the first American to join the Royal Air Force, was killed on August 16, 1940.

Q. Identify the British general who was killed in a plane crash and is buried in Arlington National Cemetery in the U.S.

A. Major General Orde Wingate, who along with several Americans died on March 24, 1944, in Burma. Because identification was impossible, all of the victims were buried in a common grave at Arlington.

FACT U.S. General Henry H. Arnold learned how to fly from the Wright brothers. He was the first five-star general in the Army Air Force and among the first five fliers in the Army Air Corps.

Q. Identify the Luftwaffe ace who had a likeness of Mickey Mouse painted on his fighter.

A. Adolf Galland. He was one of thirty-eight German aces to score more than 100 "kills." His personal score was 103. The practice of naming aircraft and illustrating the names with art was common to both Allied and Axis air forces. The two U.S. bombers in photos above were at Fenton Field, Australia. Harold D. Zahler, who took the previous photo of *SNAFU II* and the one of *Satan's Secretary*, managed to have himself snapped next to *Puss & Boots*.

Exclusive Photos by Harold D. Zahler

Q. Identify the most decorated bomber pilot in the Luftwaffe.
  a. Gerhard Barkhorn
  b. Werner Baumbach
  c. Heinz Wodarczyk
A. Oberleutnant Werner Baumbach, who at one time was the commander of the dreaded Kampfgeschwader 200 (KG 200), the Luftwaffe organization that flew captured U.S. and British aircraft. Barkhorn was Germany's second-leading fighter ace (with 301 kills), while Wodarczyk was one of two Luftwaffe pilots who managed to attack Allied troops during D-Day. The other was "Pips" Priller. (Volume 1, page 215)

Q. Name the three Japanese cities that were targets of the final air raid of the war.
A. The three cities bombed by U.S. B-29s were Kumagaya, Isesaki and Akita. The raid took place on August 14, 1945, the same day Japan agreed to surrender unconditionally.

Q. Identify the first British aircraft type to be shot down in the war.
A. A Wellington bomber on September 7, 1639, while it was preparing to bomb the German battle cruiser *Gneisenau*.

Q. Identify the Polish fighter plane that was never used by the Polish but was purchased by the air forces of Greece, Bulgaria, Turkey and Rumania.
A. The P.Z.L. P-24f, first produced in 1634.

Q. Where was the first major training ground of U.S. airborne pathfinder units?
A. At Biscari Airfield in Sicily.

FACT U.S. Army Air Force personnel assigned as heavy bomber crews fought odds of nine to one that they would become casualties in the European Theater of Operations. Casualty rates for heavy bomber crews were almost three times as great as for medium bomber crews and just under twice the rate of casualties sustained by fighter pilots.

FACT German fighter planes shot down or damaged 145 out of 178 Allied planes that attacked the oil refineries in German-occupied Rumania on August 1, 1943. Of the 1,733 U.S. personnel flying the B-24s, 446 were killed. Only thirty-three of the planes ever saw combat again.

Q. Name the American B-24 Liberator that was found in a state of near perfect preservation in the Libyan desert in May 1959.

A. The *Lady Be Good*, which was reported missing on April 4, 1943. It was first sighted on November 9, 1958, from the air by geologists Ronald McLean and S. V. Sykes. After apparently overshooting their base, the crew was forced to land in the desert when their fuel expired. They perished as they were making their way across the desert on foot. Remarkable photo above captures the instant of a flak burst as seen from the top turret of a B-24 Liberator en route to raid the Ploesti oil fields in Rumania. Plane in photo is from Group 456, Squad 746, Fifteenth Air Force.

Exclusive Photo from Mrs. Kenneth L. Boughner

Q. Identify the last U.S. aircraft type involved in action in the war.

A. Although the war with Japan ended August 15, 1945 (but September 2 is celebrated as VJ-Day since that is when the surrender was signed), a B-32 aircraft on a photo reconnaissance mission over Japan on August 18 was engaged by Japanese fighters. One U.S. airman was killed and two others were wounded. The B-32 involved was named *Hobo Queen II*. (Volume 1, page 140)

Q. When did U.S. Marine Corps pilots shoot down their first and last enemy planes in the war?

A. Japanese planes at Wake Island were the first, and Japanese planes at Okinawa were the last. Between those battles, USMC pilots scored 2,355 "kills," which resulted in 121 aces, including five who scored twenty or more "kills."

Q. Besides the December 7, 1941, attack on Pearl Harbor, when else did Japanese aircraft bomb the Hawaiian Islands during the war?

A. On March 5, 1942, three Kawanishi H8K2 flying boats, unable to locate Pearl Harbor, dropped their bombs elsewhere on Oahu. Visibility was bad.

Q. What was the reconnaissance version of the B-29 known as?

A. Produced in limited quantity toward the end of the war, it was identified as the F-13.

Q. Identify the first U.S. aviation unit to operate on Japanese soil.

A. The war with Japan ended on August 15, 1945, and the surrender was signed aboard the battleship USS *Missouri* (BB-63) in Tokyo Bay on September 2. Five days later, U.S. Marine Corps aircraft began using the airfield at Yokosuka. The particular group gaining the distinction was Marine Aircraft Group 31. No U.S. aircraft operated from Japanese homeland bases during the hostilities.

FACT Allied bomber raids against Germany suffered heavy losses between August 1942 and December 1943 for lack of adequate long-range fighter escorts. During one week in October 1943, the Allies lost 153 planes to the Germans.

Q. Identify the future U.S senator and presidential candidate who piloted
a B-24 named *Dakota Queen* in the Fifteenth Air Force.

A. George McGovern of the 455th Bomber Group. In photo above, a
"box" of B-24s wing toward the oil fields in Ploesti, Rumania.

Exclusive Photo from Mrs. Kenneth L. Boughner

Q. What was the name of the B-25 that Congressman/Lieutenant Commander Lyndon B. Johnson was aboard when it was reportedly attacked by Japanese aircraft over New Guinea?

A. *Heckling Hare.* The future President was the only person aboard
the aircraft to be awarded the Silver Star for the action. (Volume
1, page 63)

Q. Who succeeded General Hans Jeschonnek as Luftwaffe chief of staff
in 1943?

A. General Gunther Korten. (Volume 1, page 12)

Q. Who was "Sailor" Malan?

A. The South African pilot who became the third-highest ace in the
RAF with thirty-five "kills." He was the first pilot to receive both
the Distinguished Flying Cross (with bars) and the Distinguished
Service Order. His full name was Adolph G. Malan. (Volume 1, page
214)

Q. Identify the type of aircraft that Bruno Mussolini, the Italian dictator's son, was killed testing in 1639.

A. The Piaggio P-108B, a four-engine heavy bomber which was often compared to the U.S. B-17. It was Italy's only four-engine heavy bomber of the war but produced in such low quantity (fifty-five) that it had little impact.

Q. Where did the U.S. Navy planes that arrived at Pearl Harbor during the December 7, 1941, attack come from?

A. The aircraft carrier USS *Enterprise* (CV-6), which was returning from a trip to Wake Island. There were eighteen planes.

Q. Who flew the first Bloch 174 light bomber–reconnaissance aircraft into action for France against Germany?

A. French civil aviation pioneer and noted writer Antoine de Saint-Exupéry on March 29, 1940.

Q. What did Mikhail Gurevich and Artem Mikoyan contribute to the war effort?

A. They were the designers of the MiG fighter plane, which made its debut in 1940.

Q. Identify the Allied power that had the only jet fighter plane to see combat against the Luftwaffe during the war.

A. Great Britain, with its Meteor. It is reported to have entered combat nearly a month before the Messerschmitt-262 jet.

Q. Name the first five U.S. Army Air Force sergeants ever to fly in combat as pilots.

A. Despite regulations that only commissioned officers could act as pilots the following five men did fly against the Luftwaffe in 1944: John Ferguson of Bayside, New York; Dennis L. A. Johns, of Jackson, Michigan; Daniel L. Richards, of Long Beach, California; Donald E. Dempsey, of Elyria, Ohio; and William C. Arney, of Buffalo, New York.

FACT The German Messerchmitt-262 jet had a top speed of 540 miles per hour.

FACT When Japanese fighters shot off most of the right wing of this Chinese National Aviation Corporation DC-3, the company used the wing of a DC-2 to replace it and flew the plane to safety. It was promptly nicknamed the DC-2½.

McDonnell-Douglas Photo

FACT In one of the most unusual cases of revenge recorded by either side in the war, U.S. Army Air Force Lieutenant Harold Fisher plotted to locate and shoot down the Italian pilot who had shot him down in 1943 using a decoy American P-38 fighter. The U.S. plane was being used by the Italians in very much the same way the German KG-200 units used captured Allied aircraft to infiltrate Allied formations and then shoot down as many as possible. The incident so infuriated Fisher he managed to equip a B-17 with additional armament and use himself as bait for the decoy P-38. Fisher learned the name of his nemesis, Guido Rossi, and the fact that Rossi's wife was now behind Allied lines. He had her name and likeness painted on the plane's nose. A short time after Fisher began trying to bait Rossi he was successful. When Rossi began an air-to-air radio exchange with Fisher, the U.S. pilot told the Italian pilot that he named his plane after a woman he had been living with — then identified her. As Fisher expected, Rossi put his previous tactics aside and came at the B-17 directly. Fisher shot him down and Rossi was picked up and became a prisoner of war. The bizarre episode won Fisher the Distinguished Flying Cross.

Q. Identify the U.S. serviceman listed as the first American to be killed in action in the Pacific.

A. U.S. Navy Ensign Manuel Gonzalez, a pilot from the aircraft carrier USS *Enterprise* (CV-6), on December 7, 1941.

Q. What was necessary to become a member of the Goldfish Club?

A. An Allied airman who was picked out of the sea after being shot down qualified.

Q. Identify the first type of German aircraft shot down in the war.

A. A Junkers-87 Stuka during the invasion of Poland. Polish Air Force fighter pilot Wladyslaw Gnys is credited with doing it. He became a member of the RAF after fleeing from Poland.

Q. What was the name of the airstrip on Betio Island, Tarawa?
>   a. Haskins Field
>   b. Hasset Field
>   c. Hawkins Field

A. Named after USMC Medal of Honor winner Lieutenant William Hawkins, who died on Tarawa, the airstrip was Hawkins Field. (Volume 1, page 137)

Q. Who was General Dwight D. Eisenhower's pilot?

A. Captain Larry Hansen.

Q. Name the first ace in the Flying Tigers?
>   a. Claire Chennault
>   b. Richard Bong
>   c. Duke Hedman

A. Duke Hedman, who scored his five "kills" on December 25, 1941.

FACT The world-famous Baedeker travel guide books were used by the Luftwaffe to select important targets for bombing in Britain. They publicly announced that buildings that Baedeker had given three stars to would be primary targets. German troops also used Baedeker guides during land campaigns in Europe in areas where their military maps were incomplete. (Volume 1, page 164)

Q. Name the U.S. Army Air Force officer who defected to Germany in order to fight the Soviets.

A. Lieutenant Martin J. Monti, who crossed sides in October 1944 by flying his fighter to Vienna. The Nazis accepted him but rather than letting him join the Luftwaffe they gave him command of an SS unit made up largely of Americans. After the war Monti was tried for treason and given a twenty-five-year prison term.

Q. What was the Allied code name for the air raids on the Benedictine Abbey at Cassino in March 1944?
      a. Operation Hemingway
      b. Operation Deighton
      c. Operation Ludlum
      d. Operation Uris

A. Operation Ludlum, which was named after the USAAF officer who signaled the attack after several postponements due to bad weather.

Q. Who was the commander of Luftflotte 3 on the Western Front in 1944?

A. General Field Marshal Hugo Sperrle.

Q. How many tons of bombs did Britain drop on Germany?

A. Just over 645,920 tons.

Q. How many air raids did Berlin sustain during the war?

A. The British and American air forces conducted 363 raids over a period of three years and eight months.

FACT If it became necessary to drop a third atom bomb on Japan, the city that would have been the target was Tokyo. On August 10, 1945, the day after the bomb was dropped on Nagasaki, U.S. planes dropped counterfeit Japanese yen warning that a third bomb would be dropped unless Japan surrendered. The obverse of the money was authentic-looking while the reverse side carried the third-bomb message. Tokyo was not mentioned as the intended target. This view of Tokyo is from the top of the Finance Building looking toward the Imperial Palace (extreme left) and the Daitchi Building (center).

Exclusive Photo by George Schroth

Q. What was the nickname of the C-47?

A. The Gooney Bird. The C-47 and the other derivative of the DC-3, the R4D, were the mainstay of the U.S. Carrier Command and served as troop and cargo transports, hospital ships and also as bombers and gliders.

McDonnell-Douglas Photo

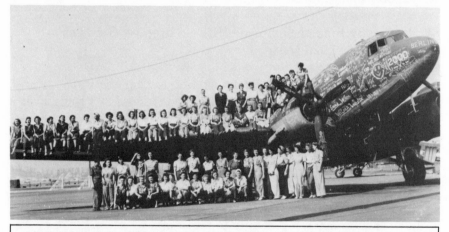

FACT The C-47 military version of the DC-3 was produced at a rate of 1.8 aircraft per hour at the peak of mass production. In total, Douglas Aircraft (now McDonnell-Douglas) produced 10,196 C-47s at plants in California and Oklahoma. In photo above the seventy-one female assemblers who worked on the 2,000th plane in Long Beach took time to sign it and get their picture taken.

McDonnell-Douglas Photo

Q. Identify the Japanese aircraft that was almost an exact duplicate of the U.S. DC-3.
A. The L2D.

Q. Who was the highest-scoring ace in the Flying Tigers?
　　a. Richard Bong
　·b. Pappy Boyington
　　c. Bob Neale
　　d. Claire Chennault
A. Neale, who scored sixteen "kills" while a member of the Flying Tigers.

Q. Identify the mountain in Oregon that was hit by bombs dropped by a Japanese plane.
A. Mount Emily, on September 9, 1942, by Lieutenant Nobuo Fujita. He was launched by catapult from the submarine I-25. He is the only military member of a foreign power to have done this during the war. (Volume 1, page 160)

Q. Name the Japanese prisoner of war camp where VIP prisoners, including Pappy Boyington, were held.
A. Ofuna.

Q. Who was the commander in chief of the Soviet Air Force?
A. Marshal Alexander A. Novikov.

Q. What was deflection shooting?
A. The art of squirting gunfire ahead of an enemy aircraft. Its success depended on hair-trigger judgment of the angles, speeds and distances that separated two planes traveling in different directions at more than six miles per minute.

Q. Who was France's top air ace of the war?
A. Marcel Albert, with twenty-three "kills."

FACT U.S. Navy fighter ace Lieutenant Edward (Butch) O'Hare was killed in action by friendly fire. He was mistaken by the rear gunner of a TBF for Japanese during a night mission and was shot down. (Volume 1, page 138)

Q. Identify the first German city to be hit by 4,000-pound bombs.
A. Emden, on March 31, 1941.

Q. Besides the Ju-87 Stukas, identify the other two German aircraft that dominated the skies over Poland in 1639.
A. Two medium bombers, the Dornier Do-17 and the Heinkel He-111.

Q. What were British and German air losses during the evacuation of Dunkirk?
A. The RAF lost 106 planes vs. 156 for Germany.

Q. Where and when was the first RAF 1,000-plane raid on a German city?
A. May 1942, when 1,130 planes hit Cologne.

Q. Where did Britain suffer its first civilian casualties as a result of a German air raid?
A. In the Orkney Islands on March 16, 1940, when the Luftwaffe bombed the location.

Q. When did the Allied "fire raid" on Hamburg take place?
A. July 1943.

Q. Who was the top Soviet air ace in the war?
A. Major Ivan N. Khozedub with sixty-two "kills."

Q. Who was Norway's top ace of the war?
A. Svein Heglund, with fifteen "kills" while a member of the RAF.

Q. Who was the top Yugoslavian air ace of the war?
A. Critan Galic, with thirty-six "kills." (Author's note: he was inadvertently omitted from list of the top aces that appears in Volume 1, page 214.)

Q. What was the nickname of the version of the C-47 (DC-3) that had 41-foot-long pontoons?
A. The Duck. The tremendous pontoons on the amphibious transport were the longest ever made.

McDonnell-Douglas Photo

Q. Where did the Japanese surrender delegation first come in physical contact with American forces?

A. On Ie Shima in August 1945 when several members of the advance delegation landed there to make preparations for the actual surrender. In top photo the delegation is met by unidentified American military personnel. In bottom photo flight crews from Japanese Betty bombers pose with an American interpreter (front row, second from left).

Photos by George M. Barclay

Naval Operations and Sea Battles

Q. Who was Isoroku Takano?

A. Born on April 4, 1884, Isoroku Takano was thirty-two years old when he was adopted into another Japanese family (as was the custom in order to prevent a family name from dying if there were no male heirs). His name, Isoroku, is spelled with the ideographs of the numbers 56, which was the age of his natural father when Isoroku was born, and they indicated the pride the older man had in fathering a son at that age. With his adoption, Isoroku took the name of his new family and, in so doing, guaranteed it a place in Japanese world history. As Isoroku Yamamoto he will be remembered as one of Japan's greatest admirals.

Q. Identify the only U.S. Navy officer ever to be court-martialed for losing a ship in war.

A. Captain Charles McVay, commanding officer of the cruiser USS *Indianapolis*, which was sunk on July 30, 1945, by Japanese submarine I-58. It was the greatest loss of life (883) on the high seas ever sustained by the U.S. Navy.

Q. Identify the famous naval battle incorrectly named for a location other than where it was actually fought.

    a. Leyte Gulf
    b. Coral Sea
    c. Philippine Sea

A. The Battle of the Coral Sea was not fought there but rather in the Solomon Sea, on May 7 and 8, 1942. It was Japan's first defeat of the war. (Volume 1, pages 31, 171 and 173)

Q. Identify the German U-boat captain who attempted to sink the luxury liner *Queen Elizabeth*.
A. Horst Kessler of U-704. (Volume 1, page 57)

Q. Identify the four chaplains who gave up their life preservers to troops on the SS *Dorchester* as she sank in 1942.
A. George L. Fox, Clark V. Poling, John P. Washington and Alexander D. Goode.

Q. Name the twelve-year-old boy who managed to enlist in the U.S. Navy and served on the battleship USS *South Dakota* (BB-57).
A. Calvin Graham, who won a Bronze Star and a Purple Heart before the Navy found out how old he was, served aboard the battleship nicknamed Old Nameless.

Q. Name the only Japanese battleship to survive the war.
A. The 42,785-ton *Nagato*. The 725-foot-long warship was the nineteenth largest battleship in the war. (Volume 1, page 210).

Q. Name the only German aircraft carrier in the war years.
A. The *Graf Zeppelin*. Its keel was laid in 1938, but the ship was not finished before the end of the war and it did not see action.

Q. Identify the only British aircraft carrier to make it through the war.
A. HMS *Furious*, which was originally a cruiser and then converted to a carrier.

Q. Identify the ships' bands who were finalists Saturday night, December 6, 1941, in "The Battle of Music" at Pearl Harbor.
A. The bands from the following ships: USS *Pennsylvania*, USS *Tennessee*, USS *Argonne* and USS *Detroit*. The *Arizona*'s band had been eliminated.

Q. Where were Japan's midget submarines designed and made?
A. They were designed in Germany but built in Japan. In photo, a midget sub captured at Pearl Harbor is seen on display in New York City's Times Square during the war.

Exclusive Photo by George Schroth

Q. Who said, "There will always be an *England* in the U.S. Navy"?
A. U.S. Admiral Ernest King, with reference to the destroyer escort USS *England* that sank six Japanese submarines in twelve days and was seriously damaged by kamikazes off Okinawa in 1945. In photo above, Admiral King is seen at the Red Arrow in London on June 15, 1944.

U.S. Army Photo

> **FACT** The first ship sunk in the war, the Cunard Line's *Athenia*, was featured in the movie *Arise My Love*.

Q. Identify the U.S. ship that sank five enemy submarines in eight days.

A. The destroyer escort USS *England*, under the command of Lieutenant Commander W. B. Pendleton in May 1944 in the Pacific. Actually Pendleton's ship totaled six subs during the last twelve days of the month.

Q. When was the first U.S. submarine sunk in the Atlantic?

A. On January 24, 1942, the S-26 was rammed and sunk off Panama.

Q. Although the "social consumption of alcoholic beverages" was strictly prohibited aboard all U.S. Navy ships, it was a regulation that was often and easily circumvented. What did the submariners call their supply of spirits (allegedly intended for medicinal use)?

A. Depth-charge whiskey. Most veterans of the Silent Service remember their boats having a good supply on hand.

Q. Name the U-boat commander who sank the British passenger liner *Athenia* in September 1939:
   a. Otto Kretschmer
   b. Fritz Lemp
   c. Erich Topp
   d. Gunther Prien

A. Lieutenant Fritz Lemp. The others are the first-, fourth-, and eighth-highest-scoring U-boat commanders, respectively. (Volume 1, page 212)

> **FACT** The magnitude of Hitler's crimes against humanity are historically documented. However, one incident for which he was blamed by Allied propagandists is in fact false. The sinking of the British liner *Athenia* on the first day of war (September 1, 1939) was an act contrary to his orders not to attack passenger liners. The embarrassing mistake by U-30 resulted in German propagandists turning the tables and blaming the sinking on the British themselves.

FACT According to JANAC (Joint Army-Navy Assessment Committee), the official investigating team that tallied losses at the end of the war, U.S. forces sank approximately 10 million tons of Japanese shipping, including 8 million tons of merchant ships. U.S. submarines sank more than half of the combined tonnage, precisely 54.6 percent, for 5.3 million tons (1,314 ships). Land-based and carrier aircraft were credited with a third of the total (929 ships for 3 million tons), while the remaining 1.4 million tons were sunk by surface craft, mines and miscellaneous causes.

FACT The last ship present at Pearl Harbor on December 7, 1941, to be sunk in hostile action was the former USS *Phoenix* (CL-46), which the U.S. sold to Argentina in 1951. Renamed the *General Belgrano*, she was sunk by a British submarine on May 2, 1982, off the Falkland Islands during the conflict between those two nations. In this February 28, 1944, photo, Vice Admiral Thomas C. Kinkaid and General Douglas MacArthur are seen on the flag bridge of the *Phoenix* during the bombardment of Los Negros Island. Colonel Lloyd Lehrbas, an aide to MacArthur, is at extreme right. Photo was taken by Pfc. Gae Falilace.

U.S. Army Photo

Q. Name two submarines that sank Soviet ships by mistake during the war.

A. In February 1943 the USS *Sawfish* sank the *Kola* and the *Ilmen*, while in May of that year the USS *Sundlance* sank the *Bella Russa*. In all three sinkings, the Soviet ships were mistaken for Japanese.

Q. Name the U.S. submarine that incorrectly identified the Navy salvage ship USS *Extractor* and sank her on January 23, 1945.

A. The USS *Guardfish*.

Q. Who was the only U.S. submarine skipper relieved of command of a *Japanese* submarine for cause?

A. Hiram Cassedy, who had been assigned to accept the surrender at sea of one of three I-class subs designed and built to torpedo the Panama Canal. He violated strict orders not to take souvenirs by passing out Japanese swords. Admiral William Halsey removed him from command.

Q. What distinction does British Royal Navy Captain Donald Macintyre hold?

A. A prominent U-boat hunter, Captain Macintyre captured Germany's most successful U-boat commander ever, Otto Kretschmer, in March 1941. As commander of U-23 and U-99, Kretschmer sank forty-five ships during sixteen patrols. (Volume 1, page 212)

Q. How was the USS *Juneau* sunk?

A. By torpedoes from Japanese submarine I-26. The *Juneau* was the ship on which the five Sullivan brothers perished. (Volume 1, page 177)

FACT For every U.S. surface-ship sailor lost in the war, six U.S. submariners lost their lives. Although the 1,700 U.S. submarine war patrols were responsible for more than half of Japan's sea losses (nearly one half million Japanese), the cost in U.S. lives was the heaviest ratio of any branch of the U.S. armed forces, including the Marines. One out of every seven U.S. submariners died — 3,505 officers and enlisted men and one out of every five submarines was lost. In the Pacific forty-nine were sunk and in the Atlantic three. (Volume 1, pages 174-175)

FACT The first U.S. Navy PT boat, #9, arrived in New York from Great Britain two days after World War II had begun in September 1939. It had been purchased there by Henry R. Sutphen, executive vice president of the Electric Boat Company, which had its Elco Naval Division in Bayonne, New Jersey. The Navy took delivery of its first boat (PT #9) in June 1940 from Elco. By the time Pearl Harbor was attacked, several manufacturers were offering designs in what were called the Plywood Derbys of 1941. Sutphen used his British-purchased boat as a model for the hundreds of others made at the Elco facility.

Author's Collection

Q. Identify the U.S. submarine that has the distinction of sinking three enemy submarines in as many days.

    a. USS *Tang*

    b. USS *Batfish*

    c. USS *Ling*

A. In February 1945, on her sixth war patrol, the USS *Batfish* encountered three of the four known Japanese submarines around the Philippines and sank them in three days. No other submarine of any navy had done that before, or since. *Batfish* is now a memorial exhibit in Muskogee, Oklahoma, while USS *Ling* is on exhibit in Hackensack, New Jersey. (See Appendix.)

Q. Name the only U.S. submarine credited with sinking a battleship in the war and name the battleship.

A. The USS *Sealion II* sank the Japanese battleship *Kongo* off Foochow, China, on November 21, 1944. The American submarine was under the command of Commander G. T. Reich.

Q. Identify the U.S. submarine credited with sinking the first Japanese destroyer in the war.

A. The SS-44, which sank the *Kako* on August 10, 1942.

Q. Identify the first submarine sunk by aircraft fire during the war.

A. The Italian submarine *Argonauta*, on June 28, 1940, by a British Sunderland.

Q. Name the first Japanese submarine sunk by aircraft fire in the war.

A. The I-70 on December 10, 1941, by planes from the USS *Enterprise* (CV-6).

FACT German naval hero and U-boat captain Gunther Prien sank a 15,500-ton British passenger ship, the *Arandora Star*, in July 1940, some nine months after his daring penetration of Scapa Flow and subsequent sinking of the battleship HMS *Royal Oak*. While his action against the British at Scapa Flow did much to raise German morale, his sinking of the *Arandora Star* had a reverse effect. The British ship was transporting some 1,500 German and Italian prisoners to Canada. (Volume 1, page 164)

Q. Of the ten armed merchantmen that Germany used on the high seas during the war, which was the last one to survive?

A. The *Michel*, which was sunk by the submarine USS *Tarpon* off Japan in October 1943. Merchantmen raiders accounted for 133 Allied ship sinkings, totaling 830,000 tons. Only one of the ten was charged with actions not permitted by international law or the rules of war, and its captain was tried as a war criminal.

Q. Identify the first member of the U.S. Submarine Service to win the Medal of Honor.

A. Commander Howard Gilmore, CO of the USS *Growler* was posthumously given the award in 1943. Gilmore ordered his officers to clear the bridge of the submarine while he remained on deck to maneuver the *Growler* to safety after it had rammed a Japanese gunboat. Injured in the exchange of gunfire that followed, Gilmore gave his last order to the officer of the deck: "Take her down." The *Growler* dived, seriously damaged, and escaped to safety. Commander Gilmore remained topside.

Q. Name the first Japanese submarine to be sunk as a result of Hedgehog, or cluster bomb, fire.

A. The I-175 on February 5, 1944. Hedgehogs, and a smaller version called Mousetraps, were adopted by the U.S. Navy in 1942. They consisted of clusters of bombs that broke into a pattern after being fired from a surface ship.

Q. Name the Japanese submarine that sank off Truk as a result of a sailor failing to secure one of its torpedo doors.

A. The I-169 which was forced to perform an emergency dive from attacking U.S. planes. The sub crew perished after several unsuccessful efforts to refloat her.

FACT Germany's second-highest-scoring U-boat captain, Wolfgang Luth, was accidentally shot and killed by a sentry for failing to properly identify himself near the headquarters of Admiral Karl Doenitz. Luth commanded four different U-boats in the war, made fourteen patrols and sank forty-four enemy ships, just one short of tying Otto Kretschmer's record.

> **FACT** Twenty percent of the German U-boat fleet was lost as a result of British air and naval fire in March 1941. The German casualties included several veteran U-boat commanders.

Q. Identify the first U.S. ship sunk on the high seas by a Japanese submarine.

A. The SS *Cynthia Olson*, approximately 750 miles from the West Coast on December 7, 1941, by submarine I-26.

Q. Identify the German U-boat credited with sinking the first Allied warship, HMS *Courageous*, in the war.

A. U-29, under the command of Otto Schuhart, sank the aircraft carrier on September 17, 1939. Royal Navy records note that 519 members of the 22,500-ton ship's crew perished.

Q. Identify the only U.S. submarine sunk by a Japanese submarine in the war.

A. The USS *Corvina* on November 16, 1943, off Truk by the I-176.

Q. Identify the first U.S. submarine to sink a Japanese submarine in the war.

A. The USS *Gudgeon*, under the command of Lieutenant Commander Joseph Grenfell, sank the I-173 on January 27, 1942. Another skipper of this boat, William S. Post, Jr., recorded the fifth-highest number of enemy ships sunk (nineteen) between his service on the *Gudgeon* and the USS *Spot*. (Volume 1, page 213)

Q. Name the U.S. submarine credited with sinking the last Japanese submarine in the war.

A. The USS *Spikefish*, which sank the I-373 on August 13, 1945, two days before the war ended. Japan lost over 130 submarines as opposed to 52 lost by the U.S. in the war. (Volume 1, pages 174,175)

Q. Name the U.S. submarine that fired the last torpedo and is credited with sinking the last Japanese combatant ship in the war, on August 14, 1945.

A. The USS *Torsk* (AG SS-423), which was commissioned in December 1944. In 1972, she became a submarine memorial and is open to the public at Baltimore, Maryland.

> **FACT** Japanese kamikaze and Tokko Tai suicide planes sank thirty-four
> U.S. ships at a cost of 1,228 pilots for Japan.

Q. Identify the two submarines involved in the only U.S. underwater collision of the war.

A. The USS *Hoe* and USS *Flounder* apparently needed more room to navigate than they had off Indochina and managed to make contact on February 23, 1945. Neither sub sank.

Q. Identify the Japanese ship credited with sinking the aircraft carrier USS *Wasp* (CV-7).

A. Submarine I-19 hit the *Wasp* with torpedoes near Espiritu Santo on September 15, 1942, and the carrier had to be finished off by friendly fire from U.S. destroyers. Commander of the I-19 was Takaichi Kinashi, Japan's leading submarine commander. (Volume 1, page 179)

Q. Identify the first U.S. ship to be sunk in U.S. coastal waters in the war.

A. The USS *Jacob Jones*, a destroyer, off New Jersey on February 28, 1942. It was torpedoed by U-578.

Q. Identify the only U.S. ship sunk by the Japanese Kaitens (human suicide torpedoes).

A. The SS *Mississinewa* in October 1944.

Q. Identify the future U.S. President who was director of physical education aboard the aircraft carrier USS *Monterey*:

    a. John F. Kennedy

    b. Lyndon B. Johnson

    c. Richard M. Nixon

    d. Gerald R. Ford

    e. Jimmy Carter

A. It was Gerald R. Ford. He was also the carrier's assistant navigation officer. All five of the above choices were Navy men and served as President *consecutively* after Dwight D. Eisenhower, an Army man.

Q. Which country lost the greatest number of hospital ships during the war?

A. Italy, which lost eight.

Q. Name the first U.S. Navy ship designated as an escort aircraft carrier, or baby flattop.

A. The converted cargo ship SS *Mormacmail* became the USS *Long Island*.

Q. Identify the U.S. Navy admiral who holds the unfortunate distinction of having two aircraft carriers lost while he was aboard them.

A. Admiral Frank J. Fletcher, winner of the Medal of Honor in 1914 for the Vera Cruz campaign, lost the USS *Yorktown* (CV-5) and USS *Lexington* (CV-2).

Q. Identify the last Japanese admiral to command a major force against the U.S. Navy in the war.

A. Admiral Seiichi Ito, who led a ten-ship action against the U.S. during the Okinawa campaign in April 1945. He was killed aboard his flagship the 72,809-ton battleship *Yamato*. (Volume 1, page 210)

Q. Identify the two U.S. admirals with the same last name who participated in the war in the Pacific.

A. Admirals Clifton Sprague and Thomas Sprague.

Q. Identify the ship that holds the record for wartime crossings of the Atlantic.

A. The Norwegian flag cargo ship *Mosdale*. It made the dangerous crossing ninety-eight times.

FACT Japan lost a total of twelve aircraft carriers in four naval battles: Coral Sea, May 7–8, 1942; Midway, June 3–6, 1942; Marianas, June 18–20, 1944; and Leyte, October 23–26, 1944. These losses are considered critical in the reversal of Japan's supremacy of the skies in the Pacific. At the outbreak of war, December 7, 1941, Japan had over 3,500 aircraft vs. fewer than 1,300 Allied aircraft in the war area. The U.S. lost three aircraft carriers in the same four battles.

> **FACT** During her forty months of combat in the war the USS *North Carolina* (BB-55) was reported sunk six times by Japanese propagandists, the USS *South Dakota* (BB-57) five times.

Q. Identify the first U.S. battleship to launch an aircraft from her decks. (Note: This took place *pre*-World War II).

A. The USS *Texas* (BB-35), which is a veteran of both world wars. Commissioned in 1914, she became a state shrine in 1948, the first battleship so designated by a state, and is open to the public at San Jacinto State Park, Texas.

Q. Identify the only U.S. battleship to sink a Japanese battleship in the war.

A. The USS *Washington* (BB-56), which sank the *Kirishima* on November 15, 1944, off Savo Island in the Solomons.

Q. Identify the two Japanese battleships that participated with the fleet that attacked Pearl Harbor.

A. *Hiei* and *Kirishima*. In all there were thirty-one ships in the attack fleet.

Q. Identify the U.S. Navy ship that President Franklin Roosevelt traveled on for the Middle East conferences in Cairo and Teheran.

    a. *Augusta*
    b. *Iowa*
    c. *Missouri*

A. The battleship USS *Iowa* (BB-61).

Q. Identify the only state in the U.S. that has never had a battleship named after it.

A. Montana. Work was started on a battleship to be named USS *Montana* for World War I, and in World War II a *Montana*-class was also begun, but in both cases the wars ended before the ships were built and christened.

> **Q.** Identify the only U.S. warship that was present both at Pearl Harbor on December 7, 1941, and at Normandy on D-Day, June 6, 1944.
> **A.** The battleship USS *Nevada* (BB-36). In photo at left, she is settling and burning at Pearl Harbor. Note fireboat alongside.
>
> *U.S. Navy Photo*

FACT A mission from the Japanese Naval Air Force visited Taranto in May 1941 and was given a detailed account of how aircraft from British carriers had attacked the Italian ships there. It is highly likely that what they learned was used in Pearl Harbor.

Q. Identify the U.S. warship nicknamed the *Mighty Moo*.
A. The aircraft carrier USS *Cowpens* (CVL-25). The *Mighty Mo* was the battleship USS *Missouri* (BB-63).

Q. Who was the commander of the battleship USS *Missouri* (BB-63) during the Japanese surrender ceremonies in Tokyo Bay?
A. Captain Murry S. Stuart.

Q. Identify the U.S. warship that transported the Japanese surrender delegation from Tokyo to the USS *Missouri* (BB-63).
A. The destroyer USS *Lansdowne*.

Q. Identify the first battleship to be sunk by an attack from dive-bombing planes.
     a. HMS *Ark Royal*
     b. USS *Arizona*
     c. *Marat* (USSR)
A. The Soviet battleship *Marat* was sunk by German dive-bombers while in the port of Kronstadt in September 1941.

Q. Name the U.S. ship credited with firing the first and last American 16-inch shells in the war.
A. The USS *Massachusetts* (BB-59). The first was fired in November 1942 during Operation Torch and the last in 1945 at Honshu, Japan. She is now part of the warships exhibit open to the public at Battleship Cove, Fall River, Massachusetts.

Q. Who was the commanding officer of the German battleship *Bismarck*?
     a. Hans Langsdorff
     b. Ernest Lindemann
     c. Hans Ulrich Rudel
A. Lindemann. Langsdorff was captain of the *Graf Spee*, and Rudel was a Luftwaffe air ace. (Volume 1, pages 139 and 169)

Q. Name the two most memorable actions undertaken by Force F of the British Royal Navy.

A. The sinking of the *Bismarck* and the sinking of the French fleet at Oran.

Q. What were Japanese losses as a result of sinking the British dreadnoughts *Prince of Wales* and *Repulse*?

A. It cost the Japanese three aircraft to eliminate the 35,000-ton *Prince of Wales* and the 32,000-ton *Repulse* in the Gulf of Siam.

Q. Which country launched the first successful attack on enemy ships by aircraft-carrier planes?

A. The British, with planes from the carrier *Illustrious* against the Italians at Taranto. The battleships *Conte de Cavour*, *Littorio* and *Duilio* were so badly damaged they were unable to return to action until the war was nearly over. They represented almost half of the Italian battleship fleet.

Q. Who was the last commander-in-chief of the German Navy in the war?
  a. Admiral Hans Georg von Friedeberg
  b. Admiral Karl Doenitz
  c. Admiral Erich Raeder

A. Von Friedeberg, who killed himself after signing the surrender papers.

Q. Name the Italian admiral who became chief of the Navy upon the resignation of Admiral Domenico Cavagnari.

A. Admiral Arturo Riccardi, on December 8, 1940.

Q. Who was commander-in-chief of the Soviet Navy?

A. Admiral Nikolai G. Kuznetsov.

FACT Royal Navy Captain J. C. Leach of HMS *Prince of Wales* was one of two survivors out of eleven men on her bridge when a shell from the *Bismarck* hit her on May 24, 1941. Captain Leach was less fortunate on December 10 and lost his life when the Japanese sank the *Prince of Wales* and HMS *Repulse*.

Q. Identify the U.S. destroyer that fired the coup de grace to the disabled aircraft carrier USS *Lexington* (CV-2) on May 8, 1942.
A. The USS *Phelps*.

Q. Identify the two Royal Navy personnel who are credited with defusing the first German magnetic mine discovered in the Thames estuary on November 23, 1939.
A. Lieutenant Commander J. G. D. Ouvry and Chief Petty Officer Baldwin. Between November and December 1939, fifty-nine Allied and neutral ships (203,513 tons) were sunk by the magnetic mines.

Q. Did the Allies or the Germans have superiority on the seas at the outbreak of war in 1939?
A. The Allies were by far the stronger sea force. There were 676 ships built or launched for the Allies as opposed to 130 ships for Germany.

Q. What distinction does the Liberty Ship SS *Benjamin Warner* hold?
A. She was the last Liberty Ship built. Some 2,740 others preceded her, starting with the first, SS *Patrick Henry*, in September 1941.

Q. Identify the only remaining U.S. Liberty Ship.
A. The SS *Jeremiah O'Brian*, built in May 1943. It is now a memorial in San Francisco.

Q. Name the first Liberty Ship to be launched ten days after the keel was laid.
A. SS *Joseph N. Teal*, in October 1942.

Q. Name the first black to be named captain of a U.S. Liberty Ship.
A. Captain Hugh Mulzac, who commanded the SS *Booker T. Washington*.

Q. What were the names of the Greek battleships *Kilkis* and *Lemnos* when they were in commission as part of the U.S. Navy?
A. The *Kilkis* had been the USS *Mississippi* and the *Lemnos* was the old USS *Idaho*, whose newer namesake (BB-42) is seen here on April 1, 1945, off Okinawa.

U.S. Marine Corps Photo

> **FACT** Out of the crew of 1,421 aboard HMS *Hood*, only three survived the fatal engagement with the German battleship *Bismarck*.

Q. What distinction does the Japanese heavy cruiser *Mikuma* hold?

A. It is credited with sinking the greatest number of sister Japanese ships in the war. On February 27–28, 1942, the *Mikuma* sank four Japanese transports while trying to hit the USS *Houston*.

Q. Name the first Japanese surface ship sunk in the war.

A. The destroyer *Kisaragi* at Wake Island on December 11, 1941.

Q. Name the first Japanese ship to be scuttled in the war.

A. The 36,500-ton aircraft carrier *Akagi*, which was sunk by friendly fire after receiving serious damage in the Battle of Midway. It had been the flagship during the Japanese attack on Pearl Harbor. (Volume 1, pages 161 and 183)

Q. Name the two Japanese cruisers that took part in the attack on Pearl Harbor.

A. The *Chikuma* and the *Tone*. The first was sunk off Samar, the Philippines, by ship and aircraft fire on October 25, 1944, and the second off Kure, Japan, by aircraft on July 28, 1945.

Q. Name the Australian heavy cruiser that was hit by five Japanese kamikaze planes during the Okinawa campaign yet remained in action.

A. HMAS *Australia*.

Q. Who was the first American casualty, other than Air Force, in the war in Europe?

A. Lieutenant Colonel Loren B. Hillsinger during the raid on Dieppe in 1942. He was aboard the destroyer *Berkley* and lost a leg when the ship was bombed by the Luftwaffe.

Q. Name the U.S. admiral in command of the Saipan invasion.

A. Admiral Raymond Spruance, whose 535-ship armada brought 127,000 Marine and Army troops there on June 15, 1944. Here Spruance, left, and Admirals King and Nimitz inspect the island on July 17, 1944.

U.S. Marine Corps Photo

Q. Identify the most decorated ship in U.S. Navy history.

A. The 27,000-ton aircraft carrier USS *Franklin* (CV-13), which spent several years after the war in the mothball fleet stationed at Bayonne, New Jersey, until she was decommissioned and sold for scrap in 1947. Her navigation bridge is on exhibit as a permanent memorial in Norfolk, Virginia.

Q. Identify the first U.S. Navy captain to rise through the ranks to command an aircraft carrier.

A. Captain Leslie E. Gehres, who received the Navy Cross for saving the USS *Franklin* (CV-13) after it was seriously damaged and was considered lost.

Q. Who was the captain of the USS *Hornet* (CV-8) when Colonel (later General) Jimmy Doolittle launched his famous raid on Tokyo?

A. Captain (later Admiral) Marc Mitscher. (Volume 1, page 176)

Q. Identify the other U.S. aircraft carrier that escorted the USS *Hornet* (CV-8) during the Doolittle raid.

A. The USS *Enterprise* (CV-6).

Q. Which side was able to claim victory in the Battle of the Coral Sea?

A. As far as the naval battle is concerned, the U.S. and Japan fought to a tie, each lost a carrier — the USS *Lexington* (CV-2) and the *Shoho*. However, Japan's invasion of Australia was thwarted.

Q. Name the first two U.S. aircraft carriers to be converted from battle cruiser hulls.

A. The USS *Lexington* (CV-2) and USS *Saratoga* (CV-3), as a result of language in the Washington Naval Disarmament Treaty after World War I. The U.S. was permitted to convert two existing hulls into aircraft carriers of 33,000 tons each. In reality both topped out at just over 36,000 tons when "legal" modifications were added. In photo at left, the *Sara* is seen off Iwo Jima on February 21, 1945, after being seriously damaged by seven direct bomb hits. The damage shown was caused by two kamikaze planes.

Exclusive Photo by Tom Christie

Q. What were the ships that participated in the evacuation at Dunkirk called?
A. The Mosquito Armada.

Q. Who is credited with the success of the Dunkirk evacuation in May 1940?
A. Vice Admiral Sir Bertram Ramsay. Four years later Ramsay used his talents for mobilizing ships in the execution of the Normandy invasion.

Q. How long did it take to remove Allied troops from Dunkirk?
A. The rescue fleet continually crossed the English Channel for nine days.

Q. What is considered Britain's first naval victory in the war?
A. The hunt and offensive actions against the pocket battleship *Graf Spee*.

Q. Who was the oldest officer on active duty with the Japanese Navy when hostilities began in December 1941?
A. Admiral Osami Nagano, chief of the naval general staff. He had studied at Harvard, served as an attaché in Washington and considered New York City his second home. He was sixty-two years old.

Q. U.S. Admiral William F. Halsey signed the papers awarding the Navy and Marine Corps Medal to which future President of the United States?
A. John F. Kennedy, for his heroic actions after the sinking of the PT-109. (Volume 1, pages 175, 177)

FACT During the war, U.S. Admiral William F. Halsey made a remark about riding in Tokyo on the Emperor's horse, and several western U.S. cities presented him with saddles. In photo at left, Halsey presents a saddle to the U.S. Naval Academy Museum on November 27, 1945. Happy officer in center is museum director Captain Harry A. Baldridge, and on the right is the Superintendent of the Academy, Vice Admiral Aubrey Fitch. The saddle was made by Fred Lohlein of Bools and Butler Saddlery and presented by the Chamber of Commerce of Reno, Nevada.

U.S. Naval Academy Museum Photo

Q. What ship led the first convoy to approach the Normandy beaches for the D-Day invasion?

A. The USS *Corry*, a destroyer under the command of Lieutenant Commander George D. Hoffman.

Q. Under what conditions did the German Navy lose the destroyers *Leberecht Maass* and *Max Schultz* in the North Sea on February 22, 1940?

A. Because Germany, like Italy, did not have coordinated air and sea support but instead had an "autonomous air arm," communications often did not exist. Luftwaffe Stukas bombed and sank the *Leberecht Maass* and caused the *Max Schultz* to try to escape by sailing into a minefield, which proved fatal.

Q. How many ships did Germany lose during the battle for Norway?

A. Twenty-one ships were actually sunk, including eight submarines, three cruisers and ten destroyers. Several other ships were damaged badly.

Q. Name the British destroyer that rammed the German cruiser *Hipper* off Trondheim on April 9, 1940.
    a. HMS *Glowworm*
    b. HMS *Glower*
    c. HMS *Glassfish*

A. The HMS *Glowworm*, after being fatally hit by fire from the *Hipper*, managed to ram her attacker and signal a warning that the German fleet was at sea. *Glowworm* survivors were rescued by the *Hipper*.

Q. Who commanded Halsey's Task Force 16 at Midway?

A. Rear Admiral Raymond A. Spruance, because Halsey had developed a rash and was in the hospital.

FACT According to U.S. Navy historian Admiral Samuel Eliot Morison, the nickname Bull was attached to Admiral William F. Halsey by a newsman. However, nobody who knew Halsey personally ever called him that, even though the corruption of the name Bill was not intended to be derogatory.

FACT Italian Navy Lieutenant Luigi Durand de la Penne was captured by the British after the two-man torpedo he had directed at the battleship HMS *Valiant* damaged but did not sink the warship. In 1945, with the Italians now on the side of the Allies, de la Penne was among several naval officers awarded medals for bravery. He received a medal for his action against the HMS *Valiant* in 1941. The medal was presented by Royal Navy Captain Charles Morgan, the man who had been in command of the *Valiant* at the time of de la Penne's attack.

Q. Which of the British armed services, the RAF or the Royal Navy, suffered the greater number of fatalities?

A. The Royal Navy lost 50,758 personnel, while the RAF counted 69,606 killed. The Army, however, had 144,079 killed or missing.

Q. Name the British-built destroyer that saw action as part of the German Navy.

A. *Hermes*, which the British had given to the Greeks, only to have it captured by the Germans. (Not to be confused with HMS *Hermes*, the British aircraft carrier that was the last British warship sunk in the war.)

Q. Identify the three Italian cruisers sunk by British planes during the Battle of Cape Matapan off southern Greece.

A. The *Fiume*, *Pola* and *Zara*. The Italians also lost two destroyers. Over 2,400 Italian sailors died, while the British lost one Swordfish torpedo bomber.

Q. Identify the British and German commanders who were both killed during the sea battle for Narvik, Norway, on April 10, 1940.

A. Captain B. A. W. Warburton-Lee, commander of the British 2nd Destroyer Flotilla, and Commander Paul Bonte of the German destroyer force. Both sides lost two destroyers.

Q. Identify the two old coastal defense ships of Norway that defied a German surrender demand on April 8, 1940, and were promptly blown out of the water.

A. The *Eidsvold* and the *Norge* challenged the German invasion force heading for the port of Narvik.

Q. Identify the U.S. aircraft carrier that former major-league baseball star pitcher George Earnshaw served aboard as a gunnery officer.

A. Lieutenant Commander George Earnshaw, ace right-hander for Connie Mack's Philadelphia Athletics during the late 1920s and early 1930s, served aboard the USS *Yorktown* (CV-10).

Q. Identify the only surviving U.S. destroyer of the USS *Allen M. Sumner* class.

A. The USS *Laffey* (DD-724), which is part of the famous ship display at Patriots Point Naval and Maritime Museum in Charleston, South Carolina. (See listing of WWII ship memorials in appendix.)

Q. Name the ship that carried U.S. General Douglas MacArthur back to the Philippine Islands so he could keep his promise to return.

A. The cruiser USS *Nashville*, on October 20, 1944.

Q. Pound for pound, which type of craft was the most heavily armed in the U.S. Navy fleet?

A. The swift, deadly and highly maneuverable PT boats.

Q. Identify the U.S. ship that survived the heaviest air attack of the Pacific war against a single vessel.

A. The USS *Laffey* (DD-724) which battled twenty-two attacking Japanese planes for seventy-nine minutes off Okinawa on April 16, 1945. Five kamikazes scored direct hits, as did three bombs. The *Laffey* shot down eleven of the attacking planes and suffered over 30 percent casualties.

Q. What was the purpose of Foxer devices used by merchant marine ships?

A. They caused sufficient noise to confuse German torpedoes. Towed behind ships, they made more noise than ship propellers and made acoustic torpedoes run amok.

FACT Ernie Pyle, the distinguished news correspondent who was killed on Ie Shima and buried there, now rests in the Punchbowl, Oahu, Hawaii, between two unknowns. He merited interment there not as a war correspondent but as a U.S. Navy veteran of World War I.

> **FACT** The USS *Arizona* (BB-39), considered America's most famous
> battleship and now a permanent memorial to the U.S. personnel
> who died during the December 7, 1941, attack on Pearl Harbor,
> was seen in a 1934 Hollywood movie, *Here Comes The Navy*, star-
> ring Jimmy Cagney and Pat O'Brien. (Volume 1, pages 164, 182,
> 190, 198 and 210).

Q. How many of the fifty U.S. destroyers that President Roosevelt
sent to the British actually saw service in the Royal Navy?

A. Seven of them went to the Canadian Navy, two others were manned
by Norwegian crews, leaving forty-one that the Royal Navy
crewed with British sailors.

Q. Who was the Royal Navy commander for the raid on Dieppe, France,
in August 1942?

A. Admiral John Hughes-Hallett.

Q. Identify the U.S. Navy ensign who is credited with being the first
person to sight the Japanese at Pearl Harbor.

A. Ensign R. C. McCloy, who was aboard the minesweeper USS *Con-
dor* (AMc-14) and reported seeing the conning tower of a submarine.
It turned out to be one of the midget subs and was subsequently
sunk by the destroyer USS *Ward* (DD-139). (Volume 1, pages 181
and 183)

> **FACT** Three U.S. Navy men whose names would later be linked forever
> with World War II were involved in the first successful crossing
> of the Atlantic using flying boats in 1919. Marc Mitscher, Patrick
> Bellinger and John C. Towers were members of the crews of three
> NC-4 aircraft that departed Rockaway Beach, New York, on May
> 18. Only one of the 68-foot-long planes completed the trip, and
> it was commanded by Lieutenant Commander Albert C. Reed.
> Nicknamed Nancys, the plywood and fabric craft had a wingspan
> of 128 feet, making them the largest aircraft in the world at the
> time. Years later Bellinger would tell the world America was at
> war with his famous "Air Raid Pearl Harbor, this is no drill."
> Mitscher would achieve fame as a carrier task force commander,
> and Towers would become one of the most vocal members of Con-
> gress to fight for a U.S. Navy Air Force.

─────────────────── FACT ───────────────────

Many of the key Japanese officers involved in the planning and execution of the Pearl Harbor attack on December 7 lost their lives during the war. With the exception of Minoru Genda, who was the tactical planner, and Flight Leader Mitsuo Fuchida, whose "Tora! Tora! Tora!" initiated hostilities, here is the fate of some of the others:

• *Admiral Isoroku Yamamoto*, the man who insisted that any war with the U.S. begin with the destruction of the U.S. fleet at Pearl Harbor, was aboard a plane shot down by U.S. airmen over Bougainville, April 18, 1943.

• *Vice Admiral Chuichi Nagumo*, commander-in-chief, 1st Air Fleet (the senior officer present in the attack fleet), was killed in action at Saipan.

• *Rear Admiral Tamon Yamaguchi*, commander-in-chief, 2nd Carrier Division, died aboard his aircraft carrier during the Battle of Midway.

• *Rear Admiral Matome Ugaki*, chief of staff to Yamamoto and the man who wrote the historic "Climb Mount Niitaka" message signaling the irrevocable order to attack Pearl Harbor, died piloting a kamikaze plane on the last day of the war.

• *Lieutenant Commander Kakuiche Takahashi*, leader of the dive-bombers in the first wave, was killed on May 2, 1942, in the Battle of the Coral Sea.

• *Lieutenant Commander Shigemaru Murata*, leader of the torpedo bombers in the first wave, was killed in battle at Santa Cruz, October 26-27, 1942.

• *Lieutenant Commander Takashige Egusa*, leader of the dive-bombers in the second wave, was killed over Saipan.

• *Lieutenant Commander Shigeru Itaya*, leader of the first wave of fighter planes, was shot down by mistake by Japanese Army planes over the Kuriles.

• *Lieutenant Commander Shigekazu Shimazaki*, commander of the second-wave attack force, was killed on January 9, 1945, off the Philippines.

Of the two major participants who survived, Genda went on to become a lieutenant general and later serve as a member in the upper house of the Diet (the Japanese equivalent of the U.S. Senate). Fuchida, as noted elsewhere in this volume, converted to Christianity and toured overseas extensively as a nondenominational evangelist.

Special Pearl Harbor Quiz

After the publication of the original volume of this book, we quickly discovered that the single event in the war that generated the most interest and that people seemed to be most fascinated about is the December 7, 1941, attack on Pearl Harbor. This section contains contributions from veterans, students of history and military buffs from across the U.S. who took the time to send along their particular favorites. Nearly half of the material that follows came from those sources. Additional Pearl Harbor related material is in Volume 1, pages 30, 33, 54, 59, 60, 107, 135, 139, 144, 146, 163, 164, 165, 166, 167, 168, 181, 183, 184, 185, 187, 193 and 213. In addition, the complete listing of all 145 U.S. Navy and U.S. Coast Guard ships involved appears in that volume on pages 208–209.

> Personnel of your Naval Intelligence Service should be advised that because of the fact that from past experience shows [sic] the Axis Powers often begin activities in a particular field on Saturdays and Sundays or on national holidays of the country concerned they should take steps on such days to see that proper watches and precautions are in effect.
> —An April 1, 1941 alert from U.S. Naval Intelligence, Washington.

Q. Identify the first U.S. ship in Pearl Harbor to be hit by a Japanese torpedo.
A. The USS *Oklahoma* (BB-37). The torpedo was fired by torpedo-plane pilot Inichi Goto.

Q. What was the U.S. code name for Japan prior to hostilities?
A. Orange. The term was used in practically all communications, codes and tactical planning.

FACT Commander Mitsuo Fuchida, the leader of the air attack on Pearl
Harbor with the utterance of "Tora! Tora! Tora!" was en route
to Hiroshima by plane on August 6, 1945, and saw the mushroom
cloud rise above his homeland when the U.S. dropped the atom
bomb. Fuchida was also aboard the battleship USS *Missouri*
(BB-63) to witness the surrender ceremonies the following
September. He is believed to be the only person present at *all
three* historic events. After the war he became a convert to Christianity and frequently visited the United States. This photo was
taken the day before the surrender.

Author's Collection

> **FACT** Two leading air officers in the Japanese attack on Pearl Harbor wore red underwear and red shirts in order to conceal any injuries they might sustain during the raid. Flight Leader Mitsuo Fuchida, the overall attack commander, and Lieutenant Commander Shigemaru Murata, leader of the torpedo bombers in the first wave, reasoned that if they became wounded their blood would not show up against the red. Their intention was to prevent demoralizing other flying officers.

Q. Identify the Japanese officer involved in the Pearl Harbor attack who admired Adolf Hitler so much that he grew a toothbrush mustache.

A. The man whose "Tora! Tora! Tora!" signaled the start of the attack, Commander Mitsuo Fuchida.

Q. Identify the last U.S. ship to sortie in Pearl Harbor on December 7, 1941.

A. The cruiser USS *St. Louis* (CL-49), which ran at twenty-two knots in an eight-knot zone in order to clear the channel at 10:04 A.M. She immediately had to take evasive action to avoid two torpedoes fired from a Japanese midget submarine. The fish struck the coral reef near the channel entrance, and *St. Louis* returned fire at the sub, believing they hit the conning tower.

Q. Identify the bandleader aboard the USS *Nevada* (BB-36) who conducted his musicians through the final notes of "The Star Spangled Banner" while under attack in Pearl Harbor.

A. Oden McMillan, who reportedly picked up the tempo somewhat as enemy fire hit the ship.

Q. What was the Japanese name for its formidable Pearl Harbor strike force?

A. Kido Butai.

Q. Who was the second-highest-ranking U.S. Navy officer stationed at Pearl Harbor on December 7?

A. Vice Admiral William Satterlee Pye, outranked only by Admiral Husband E. Kimmel. While in the War Plans Division in Washington, Pye drafted the U.S. Navy's war plan for the Pacific.

Q. Identify the American who captured the first prisoner of war after the attack on Pearl Harbor, and name the prisoner.

A. U.S. Army Sergeant David M. Akui captured the commander of a midget submarine that had difficulties and drifted near the Kaneohe-Bellows Field area of Oahu, Hawaii, on December 7, 1941. Unsuccessful in an effort to scuttle the boat, and weakened from exhaustion, Ensign Kazuo Sakamaki passed out in the water and awoke on a beach with Sergeant Akui standing over him. The incident took place late in the evening of the attack, making Sakamaki prisoner of war #1.

Q. Identify the Japanese admiral who was nicknamed King Kong by his own sailors.

A. Rear Admiral Chuichi Hara, commander of the Fifth Carrier Division, which included the aircraft carriers *Shokaku* and *Zuikaku*. He was one of three carrier division commanders who participated in the attack on Pearl Harbor.

Q. After the deaths of Admiral Kidd and Captain Van Valkenburgh aboard the USS *Arizona* (BB-39), who issued the order to abandon ship?

A. Lieutenant Commander Samuel G. Fuqua.

FACT The Imperial Japanese Navy General Staff, under Admiral Osami Nagano, opposed Admiral Yamamoto's plan to attack Pearl Harbor as being too risky and continued to question Yamamoto up to the very last minute as to whether he could be sure the U.S. fleet would be there. It was the powerful and confident personage of Yamamoto himself that conquered any fears and managed to get the IJN General Staff to permit executing the attack. However, this was all predicated upon the fact that Japan continued to get assurances from its consulate in Oahu that the fleet remained stationed there. When the U.S. government ordered all twenty-four German consulates in the U.S. closed, plus all Italian consulates, during June 1941, Japan feared that as a member of the Tripartite Pact it would also face similar closures. It is believed that under such conditions (the lack of espionage revealing the presence of the U.S. fleet) the IJN General Staff may well have canceled Yamamoto's plan to attack Pearl Harbor. However, for several political reasons, the U.S. government did not close the Japanese consulates.

> **FACT** Joseph C. Grew was the U.S. Ambassador to Japan for nearly a decade and was the ranking member of the diplomatic corps when Pearl Harbor was attacked. Partially deaf, he never managed to master Japanese. However, his wife, Alice, spoke it fluently. She was the granddaughter of Commodore Perry.

Q. Identify the U.S. Navy ship that happened to be in the berth at Battleship Row that was usually occupied by the battleship USS *Pennsylvania* (BB-38).

A. The minelayer USS *Oglala* (CM-4) was at Dock 1010 instead of the *Pennsylvania*, which was in dry dock across the harbor. *Oglala* was outboard the cruiser USS *Helena* (CL-50). *Oglala* was the flagship of Rear Admiral William Rhea Furlong, commander of Battle Forces Pacific (service vessels), and it was Furlong who gave the order to the fleet, "All ships in harbor sortie," as the Japanese attack began.

Q. What did the following mean: *Higashi no kazeame*?

A. It is the original Japanese quote of the famous "East wind, rain" message. It was sent to Japanese Ambassador Nomura on November 29, 1941, by the Foreign Office in Tokyo. "East wind rain" meant Japanese-U.S. relations were in danger.

Q. Identify the radio station in Hawaii that, because it was broadcasting all night to guide in U.S. B-17s from the mainland, was used by the Japanese task force as a guide to Pearl Harbor, Oahu, on December 6–7, 1941.

A. Radio station KGMB, which normally did not broadcast all night.

Q. What was the name of the radar station on Oahu that sighted the Japanese planes heading for the attack on the morning of December 7?

A. Opana Mobile Radar Station. It was staffed on that day by U.S. Army privates Joseph L. Lockard and George E. Elliott. They were due to go off duty at 7 A.M. but remained later to watch an unusual blip that had just appeared. The sighting was reported to the Army's Information Center. However, Lieutenant Kermit Tyler, the pursuit officer who had the authority to "intercept enemy planes," was convinced that the blip was the flight of U.S. B-17s expected from the mainland.

Q. Who was Tadao Fuchikami?

A. The RCA motorcycle messenger in Honolulu who delivered the Western Union telegram from Washington advising General Short and Admiral Kimmel that the Japanese were issuing an ultimatum at "1 P.M. Eastern Standard Time today..." (7:30 A.M. in Honolulu). It had been received by Honolulu RCA twenty-two minutes before the attack but not delivered until four hours later. It took another three hours to decode.

Q. Besides the eight battleships in Pearl Harbor on December 7, identify the other two that Admiral Kimmel had requested be sent there earlier in the year.

A. During a meeting in The White House with President Roosevelt on June 9, 1941, Kimmel asked his Commander-in-Chief for the USS *North Carolina* (BB-55) and USS *Washington* (BB-56) since Japan at the time had more battleships in the Pacific than the U.S. did. Fortunately, FDR did not comply.

Q. Besides the attacking Japanese planes, what else hindered the efforts of the Ford Island Fire Brigade to contain or control the numerous fires?

A. When the USS *Arizona* (BB-39) sank, she settled on the island's main water lines, resulting in a complete loss of pressure.

FACT On May 12, 1941, some seven months before the Japanese attack on Pearl Harbor, the U.S. Army and Navy held what were described as "the greatest war drills ever staged" in the Hawaiian Islands. Army bombers "attacked" enemy aircraft carriers several hundred miles at sea just as one carrier was preparing to launch planes against the islands. In an ironic note a formation of twenty-one B-17s landed on Oahu from the mainland while the "attack" was under way. The war games contained many phases and options and continued for two weeks, with the U.S. forces gaining the upper hand. The Navy had held similar games involving a Pearl Harbor attack by enemy aircraft carriers in 1933 and in 1939. In the 1939 exercise, aircraft from the carrier USS *Saratoga* (CV-3) succeeded in a surprise attack on a Sunday morning. The attacking aircraft "sank" several ships at anchor in Pearl Harbor and attacked Hickam, Wheeler and Ford Island airfields before returning safely to their carrier.

> **FACT** A Gallup Poll taken in September 1941 reflected that 70 percent of the American population was willing to risk war with Japan. A poll taken in July had shown that 51 percent held that attitude.

Q. Who was the commander of the aircraft carrier USS *Enterprise* (CV-6) when it missed being in Pearl Harbor during the December 7 attack?

    a. William F. Halsey
    b. Raymond Spruance
    c. Kelly Turner
    d. George Murray

A. Captain George Murray was the commander. Admiral Halsey was also aboard.

Q. Other than the submarine contact made on the morning of December 7, what was the earliest contact U.S. forces had indicating possible hostile submarines in Hawaiian waters?

A. On December 5, the destroyers USS *Selfridge* (DD-357) and *Ralph Talbot* (DD-390) made underwater contact with what the *Talbot* commander reported as a submarine about five miles off Pearl Harbor. He requested but was denied permission to depth-charge with the explanation that it was not a sub but a blackfish. "If this is a blackfish, it has a motorboat up its stern!" he reportedly responded. That same night Admiral William F. Halsey's task force was advised that a submarine had been reported on December 4 just south of Hawaii.

Q. What distinction does U.S. Army nurse Ann Fox hold with regard to the December 7 attack on Pearl Harbor?

A. She received the first Purple Heart presented to a woman in the war as a result of injuries she received at Hickam Field.

Q. On February 11, 1941, Admiral Husband E. Kimmel, commander-in-chief of the U.S. Fleet in Hawaii, issued a letter to his command that said, in part, "a declaration of war might be preceded by —"

    a. a surprise attack on ships in Pearl Harbor
    b. a surprise submarine attack on ships in operating area
    c. a combination of these two

A. *All three* caveats were included in his letter.

> **FACT** Lieutenant Colonel Kendall (Wooch) Fielder became intelligence
> officer (G-2) on the staff of General Walter C. Short in July 1941,
> a scant five months before the Pearl Harbor attack. He had no
> prior intelligence duty and had not previously served under Short.

Q. What was the name of the annual charity dinner-dance held on Oahu
on December 6, and attended by General Short and several other
U.S. Army staff personnel?

A. Ann Etzler's Cabaret. It was staged at the Schofield Barracks Officers' Club.

Q. Identify the Roosevelt Administration Cabinet member who flew
to Pearl Harbor on December 9, 1941.

A. Secretary of the Navy Frank Knox arrived at Kaneohe Bay on
December 11. Upon returning to Washington, Knox gave FDR a
complete report of his meetings with Admiral Kimmel, General
Short and other key military personnel, plus an evaluation of the
damage.

Q. What were Japan's estimates of its own losses with regard to the
attack on Pearl Harbor?
    a. It expected less than 10 percent losses
    b. One-third of their task force
    c. Approximately 50 percent of ships and planes

A. It was estimated that one-third of the task force would be lost, but
that such a cost was necessary. In actuality not a single surface
ship was lost, but the submarine fleet did sustain losses.

Q. Who called Pearl Harbor a "God-damn mousetrap"?

A. Admiral Kimmel's predecessor, Admiral James O. Richardson,
because of its long, narrow channel entrance that required capital
ships to enter it one at a time.

> **Q.** Who said, "What a target that would make!" upon seeing the U.S.
> fleet all lit up at Pearl Harbor on the night of December 6, 1941?
> **A.** Lieutenant General Walter C. Short, the U.S. Army commander on
> Oahu, while returning home with his wife and his intelligence officer
> (G-2), Lieutenant Colonel Kendall J. Fielder, after attending a party.
>
> *U.S. Army Photo*

Q. Identify the U.S. commander who on September 20, 1941, submitted a plan calling for joint Army-Navy exercise drills to train against a potential Japanese carrier-based air attack.

A. Major General Frederick L. Martin, commander of the Hawaiian Air Force. He suggested the "games" take place November 17–22. At the time he made the request, the Japanese were themselves considering either November 16 or 23 as the date for the attack. Martin's request was not acted upon favorably.

Q. Identify the two U.S. officers who in March 1941 were charged with the task of creating a joint Army-Navy plan in the event of an attack on Oahu or U.S. fleet ships in Hawaiian waters.

A. Rear Admiral Patrick N. L. Bellinger and Major General Frederick Martin, who authored the famous Martin-Bellinger Report. Both were based in Hawaii. Among highlights of the report are observations such as

- A successful, sudden raid against our ships and naval installations on Oahu might prevent effective offensive action by our forces in the Western Pacific for a long period.
- It appears possible that Orange [the U.S. code for Japan] submarines and/or an Orange fast raiding force might arrive in Hawaiian waters with no prior warning from our intelligence service.
- Orange might send into this area one or more submarines and/or one or more fast raiding forces composed of carriers supported by fast cruisers.
- A declaration of war might be preceded by: A surprise submarine attack on ships in the operating area. A surprise attack on Oahu, including ships and installations in Pearl Harbor.
- It appears that the most likely and dangerous form of attack on Oahu would be an air attack...such an attack would most likely be launched from one or more carriers which would probably approach inside of three hundred miles.
- Any single submarine attack might indicate the presence of a considerable undiscovered surface force...
- In a dawn air attack there is a high probability that it could be delivered as a complete surprise...

> **FACT** In the 1925 novel *The Great Pacific War*, author Hector C. Bywater detailed a fictitious account of a Japanese surprise attack against the U.S. fleet at Pearl Harbor. The novel was reportedly used in the Japanese Navy War College.

Q. Where did Japanese Consul General Kiichi Gunji, based in Hawaii, get his information on the size, numbers and movements of the U.S. fleet?

A. The information he was requested to get by Tokyo regularly appeared in the news pages of Honolulu newspapers, which included the names and exact arrival and departure times of fleet ships. This data, public information in Hawaii, became classified the moment it arrived in Japan. In addition, the Japanese consulate's treasurer, Kohichi Seki, used a copy of *Jane's Fighting Ships* to scout and identify vessels of the fleet.

Q. Though much is made of the fact that the U.S. was reading Japanese codes prior to Pearl Harbor, how many Purple decoding machines did the U.S. actually have?

A. In 1941 the U.S. had only eight such machines. Four were in Washington (two each for the Army and Navy), one went to the Philippines and two were sent to London (in exchange for Ultra intelligence we were receiving from the British). That left one machine, and it was slated for Hawaii. However, Washington wanted it, and it was known that London was also interested in a third machine. At the expense of Hawaii, and as a compromise with Washington, the machine was sent to the British.

Q. What were the Japanese J codes?

A. These were what the U.S. considered lower-grade codes between the Foreign Ministry and several of its consulates, including Honolulu. The U.S. had broken and was reading them from the summer of 1940. The J codes are not to be confused with the so-called Purple Code. The significance of the J codes, particularly one known as J-19, is that the U.S. was fully aware of Tokyo's interest in the position and/or movement of the U.S. fleet based in Hawaii. In early December 1941, the Japanese consulate in Hawaii changed from the J code to the PA-K2 code.

Q. What was the "bomb plot" message?

A. A request from Tokyo to its agents on Oahu to divide the area of Pearl Harbor into a grid when referring to locations in further communication. It was intercepted by U.S. intelligence on September 24 but not translated until October 9. At the time it was considered by most U.S. military personnel involved as an example of the extreme detail the Japanese were famous for and not as a grid pattern for an attack.

Q. To whom or what did Japan credit the sinking of the battleship USS *Arizona* (BB-39)?

A. Contrary to facts, Japan first reported — and continued to report through the spring of 1942 — that the *Arizona* was sunk by one of its midget submarines. However, Japanese Petty Officer Noboru Kanai, considered the top horizontal bombardier in the Imperial Navy, is believed to have dropped the bomb that sank the USS *Arizona* (BB-39) at Pearl Harbor. Experts, however, disagree as to whether the bomb actually went down the smokestack or struck the ship in a vulnerable position. Kanai lost his life during the battle for Wake Island.

Q. How did the medical staffs at Pearl Harbor indicate which injured personnel had already been given morphine so that double injections were not given?

A. Those already injected got Mercurochrome marks on their foreheads. More than 300 casualties arrived at the medical facilities of Patrol Wing Two within the first half hour of the attack.

Q. Identify the only U.S. Navy submariner wounded in the attack on Pearl Harbor.

A. Seaman Second Class G. A. Myers, who was hit by Japanese aircraft fire while aboard the USS *Cachalot* (SS-170).

Q. How much damage did the city of Honolulu sustain in the attack on Pearl Harbor on December 7, 1941?

A. Approximately $500,000 worth of damage, which was the result of U.S. anti-aircraft fire, not Japanese bombs. Upwards of forty explosions rocked the city.

U.S. Army Photo

Q. Identify the U.S. battleship at Pearl Harbor on December 7 that had several of her manholes open (either removed or loosened) in preparation for inspection the following day.

A. The USS *California* (BB-44), flagship of Vice Admiral William S. Pye. As a result of the open manholes the *California* nearly capsized after being hit by two torpedoes. Water poured into the fuel system and cut off light and power. However, Ensign Edgar M. Fain immediately directed counterflooding measures, which are considered to have saved the ship.

Q. Why did Kichisaburo Nomura, the Japanese Ambassador to the U.S., request on August 4, 1941, that Japan send veteran diplomat Saburo Kurusu to Washington as a special envoy to assist with efforts to secure a "final attempt at peace"?

A. Kurusu, who as Japanese Ambassador to Germany signed the Tripartite Pact, was thought of with great respect and confidence in Japanese government circles. In addition, he was married to an American woman and spoke idiomatic English, affording him the guarantee that he could not be misunderstood nor misinterpret anything said to him by the Americans.

Q. Identify the communications problem the Japanese had to overcome in preparation for the attack on Pearl Harbor.

A. Prior to 1941, Japan had never had a Navy fighter plane involved in action more than 100 miles from its home base or aircraft carrier because their radiotelephone communications system was unable to function beyond that distance. Throughout the summer of 1941, Japanese Navy pilots and communications personnel had to become proficient in Morse code in order to sustain communications during the planned Pearl Harbor attack.

Q. What distinction does U.S. Navy Lieutenant William W. Outerbridge hold?

A. He was the first American to sink a Japanese warship in 1941. As commander of the destroyer USS *Ward* (DD-139), he sighted and depth-charged a Japanese midget submarine near Pearl Harbor on the morning of December 7, nearly an hour before the enemy air attack.

> **FACT** The American opinion of the Japanese prior to, and even after,
> Pearl Harbor, saw them as a backward, ignorant race. However,
> it was not commonly known that several leading Japanese officers
> had attended some of the finest universities and colleges in the
> U.S. Some Ivy League participants in the Pearl Harbor attack
> included Yamamoto and Nagano (Harvard); Yamaguchi
> (Princeton); and Arima (Yale). Likewise, in Europe, a number of
> German generals had studied at Oxford and other English
> schools.

Q. After the attack on Pearl Harbor, to what port did the Japanese
fleet return?

A. Hiroshima, on December 23, 1941.

Q. When did Japan formally declare that a state of war existed with
the U.S.?

A. At 1600 EST on December 7, 1941, Japan announced that it was
at war with the U.S. and the British Empire. This was some three
hours after the attack on Pearl Harbor.

Q. Who did Japanese Commander Minoru Genda consider the "torpedo
ace of the Japanese Navy"?

A. The man he selected to be leader of the torpedo bombers in the first
wave against Pearl Harbor, Lieutenant Commander Shigemaru
Murata.

Q. Who was Lieutenant Commander Takeshige Egusa?

A. He was the leader of the dive bombers in the second wave of the
attack on Pearl Harbor and, according to tactical planner Commander Minoru Genda, "the number-one dive-bombing pilot in all
Japan."

Q. Name the Japanese admiral who commanded the Sixth Fleet (submarines) in the Pearl Harbor attack.

A. Vice Admiral Mitsumi Shimizu.

Q. Identify the U.S. armed forces commander who pleaded with the
U.S. War Department for bombproof aircraft repair facilities on
September 10, 1941, which he called "vital to the continued func-
tioning of the Hawaiian Air Force during an attack on Oahu."

A. Lieutenant General Walter C. Short.

Q. Identify the U.S. naval officer who wrote a memorandum entitled "Steps to be Taken in Case of American-Japanese War Within the Next Twenty-Four Hours."

A. Admiral Husband E. Kimmel, CINCUS. In a meeting with aides on December 6, Kimmel updated the prophetic memo.

Q. Who sent the first message out reporting the attack on Pearl Harbor, Bellinger or Ramsey?

A. As noted in Volume 1, page 59, Rear Admiral Patrick Bellinger has been credited with the historic message: "Air raid, Pearl Harbor — This is no drill," at 7:58 A.M. Bellinger is named as the officer in Samuel Eliot Morison's *The Two-Ocean War* and Walter Lord's *Day of Infamy*. A third source that credits Admiral Bellinger is Lieutenant Colonel Eddy Bauer in the 24-volume *Illustrated World War II Encyclopedia*. However, in *At Dawn We Slept*, author Gordon Prange claims Lieutenant Commander Logan C. Ramsey sent the message out, also at 7:58, but in this message "no" is replaced by "not." It is interesting to note that Ramsey was with a Lieutenant Richard Ballinger near the radio room of the Ford Island command center at this point in the attack and reportedly ran into the room to order radiomen on duty to send out the message. There were at least two other messages, similar in content, sent over the air in the immediate minutes reported here.

Q. Who said, "The Japs wouldn't dare attack Hawaii."?

A. U.S. Army Chief of Staff General George C. Marshall, to Secretary of War Henry L. Stimson on April 23, 1941.

Q. Who was the commander of the Southeast Asia Theater?

A. Lord Louis Mountbatten, first row center, cousin of the British King. In this photo with four American officers whose names would forever be linked to December 7, 1941, Mountbatten is shown visiting the Hawaiian Islands when he was commander of the British aircraft carrier *Illustrious*. The others: General Walter C. Short, U.S. Army commander; Admiral Husband E. Kimmel, U.S. Navy commander; General Frederick L. Martin, commander of the Hawaiian Air Force; and Admiral Patrick N. L. Bellinger, whose message "Air raid Pearl Harbor. This is no drill" would be the first news of the attack to reach Washington.

U.S. Army Photo

Q. Identify the island that served as the training center for the attack on Pearl Harbor.

A. Kyushu, the southernmost of the four main Japanese islands. Ariake Bay, frequently the home of the fleet, had a resemblance to Pearl Harbor.

Q. Prior to its extensive training, why were Japan's horizontal bombers considered a poor risk, or a minimally effective force, with regard to the attack on Pearl Harbor?

A. The Japanese used a modified version of the German Boyco bombsight, critically inferior to the Norden bombsight used by the U.S. The accuracy of the Japanese Boyco depended almost totally upon the expertise of the bombardier and pilot working together as a team.

Q. Who correctly guessed that the unusual wording of the fourteen-part Japanese message breaking diplomatic relations at 1 P.M. Washington time on December 7 indicated that hostilities against Pearl Harbor were nearly certain?

A. Commander Arthur H. McCollum, Lieutenant Commander A. D. Kramer, both of Naval Intelligence, and Colonel Rufus S. Bratton of Army Intelligence. The time in Pearl Harbor would be 7:30 A.M.

Q. When did U.S. forces in the Pacific receive the "war warning" from Washington that said in part, "An aggressive move by Japan is expected within the next few days"?

A. On November 27, 1941.

Q. Who said, "If war eventuates with Japan, it is believed easily possible that hostilities would be initiated by a surprise attack upon the fleet or the naval base at Pearl Harbor"?

A. Secretary of the Navy Frank Knox in a letter to Secretary of War Henry L. Stimson on January 24, 1941, some eleven months before the attack. The letter, which was actually written by Rear Admiral Richmond Kelly Turner and approved by Admiral Stark (before being given to Knox to sign), continued: "In my opinion the inherent possibilities of a major disaster to the fleet or naval base warrant taking every step, as rapidly as can be done, that will increase the joint readiness of the Army and Navy to withstand a raid of the character mentioned above."

> **FACT** On December 2, 1941, Lieutenant Ellsworth A. Hosner and another staff member of the 12th Naval District Intelligence (San Francisco) Office detected radio signals in the Pacific they thought could be from the Japanese fleet, which had been missing since late November. Their commander, Captain Richard T. McCollough, a friend of President Roosevelt, was advised. They continued to track the signals and on December 6 established that the position was about 400 miles north of Oahu.

Q. Who said, "Hawaii would be a fine place from which to watch a Japanese-American war"?

A. Takeo Yoshikawa, a trained Japanese intelligence agent who functioned at the consulate in Hawaii under the name of Tadashi Morimura. When he made the statement to Kohichi Seki, the Japanese consulate's treasurer and the man who had reported the movements of the U.S. fleet prior to Yoshikawa's arrival there, neither man knew anything about the planned attack on Pearl Harbor.

Q. Who said, "The only real answer was for the fleet not to be in Pearl Harbor when the attack came"?

A. Admiral Husband E. Kimmel, CINCUS, to Admiral Harold R. Stark, CNO, in a meeting in Washington on June 13, 1941, attended also by Secretary of the Navy Frank Knox. Kimmel said the congestion of ships, fuel oil storage and repair facilities in Pearl Harbor invited an "attack, particularly from the air." With the fleet in port, Kimmel said, it would take at least three hours to sortie. "The only real answer was for the fleet not to be in Pearl Harbor when the attack came," he added.

Q. Who said the following about the defense of Pearl Harbor: "It must be remembered too that a single submarine attack may indicate the presence of a considerable surface force...accompanied by a carrier"?

A. Admiral Husband E. Kimmel to Rear Admiral Claude C. Bloch, the man he named as naval base defense commander for Pearl Harbor in February 1941. At 6:45 A.M on December 7, the destroyer USS *Ward* (DD-139) depth-charged and sank a Japanese submarine more than an hour before the attack. A second sub was sunk at 0700 by a Catalina flying boat.

> **FACT** The Navy and Army commanders at Pearl Harbor, Admiral Husband E. Kimmel and General Walter C. Short, assumed their commands within days of each other in February 1941. Kimmel's tour began on February 1, while Short took over on February 7.

Q. Who said, "In view of the Japanese situation, the Navy is concerned with the security of the fleet in Hawaii...They are in the situation where they must guard against a surprise or trick attack"?

A. General George C. Marshall, U.S. Army Chief of Staff to high-ranking U.S. Army staff personnel on February 25, 1941. He continued: "We also have information regarding the possible use of torpedo planes. There is the possible introduction of Japanese carrier-based planes." Eight days later Marshall urged General Walter C. Short to send him a review of the Hawaii defenses against possible air attack, calling it "a matter of first priority."

Q. Who said, "The Japanese will not go to war with the United States. We are too big, too powerful and too strong"? When?

A. Vice Admiral William Satterlee Pye, on Oahu, Hawaii, December 6, 1941. Pye was the second-highest-ranking U.S. Navy officer at Pearl Harbor.

Q. Who said, "They [Japan] will attack right here" during a conversation about Japanese intentions on December 6, 1941, in Pearl Harbor?

A. Ensign Fred Hall, the assistant communications officer aboard the USS *Vestal* (AR-4). His prophetic statement was interjected into a conversation among other officers in the wardroom. However, nobody bothered to ask him when or why the attack would take place. The following morning Hall was the officer of the deck and pulled the general quarters signal at 7:55 A.M. as the Japanese attack began.

> **Q.** What were Japanese losses in the Pearl Harbor attack?
> **A.** In terms of human life, fifty-five fliers and nine midget submariners, plus an unknown number aboard an I-class submarine. Of the 432 planes that participated in the raid, twenty-nine were downed. In this photo, Lieutenant Fusata Iida, who crashed at Kaneohe Bay, is buried with honor by U.S. military personnel on Hawaii.
>
> *U.S. Navy Photo*

> **FACT** Admiral Husband E. Kimmel came from a Kentucky family with a West Point military tradition. Upon failing to gain admittance to the Point, he tried and succeeded in being admitted to the Naval Academy, where he graduated thirteenth in a class of sixty-two. His wife was the daughter of an admiral who was the brother of Admiral Thomas C. Kinkaid. Kimmel served as an aide to the then Secretary of the Navy, Franklin D. Roosevelt, for a brief time.

Q. Who said "This means war"?

A. President Franklin D. Roosevelt, on December 6, 1941, after reading the thirteen-part message Tokyo had sent to its ambassadors in Washington. (The copy FDR read was not the official communication which would not be delivered until the following day, but the result of U.S. code-breaking activity.) The fourteenth part had not been seen by the President at this time.

Q. Who said, "To make victory certain, we would have to march into Washington and dictate the terms of peace in the White House"?

A. Taken out of context, the above statement was made by Admiral Isoroku Yamamoto in a letter to Japanese ultranationalist Ryoichi Sasakawa prior to the Pearl Harbor attack. The excerpt was later used by U.S. nationalists to foster the belief that Yamamoto intended to invade the U.S. and capture Washington, D.C. In its entirety, the paragraph was actually a sarcastic cut at Japan's extreme right. Yamamoto was telling them the U.S. was not a hollow giant. It continued: "I wonder if our politicians, among whom armchair arguments about war are being glibly bandied about in the name of state politics, have confidence as to the final outcome and are prepared to make the necessary sacrifices."

Q. Who said, "If we are going into a war, why don't we have machine guns"?

A. Major Truman H. Landon to Major General Henry H. (Hap) Arnold when he and other members of the crews of the 38th and 88th Reconnaissance squadrons were about to fly to Clark Field, the Philippines, to deliver B-17s. Arnold had said, "War is imminent. You may run into a war during your flight." The planes, which were stripped to conserve fuel, had a scheduled stop at Hickam Field, Oahu, Hawaii, on December 7, 1941.

Q. Who said, "Our most likely enemy, Orange [Japan], can probably employ a maximum of six carriers against Oahu"?

A. Colonel William E. Farthing, commander of the Fifth Bombardment Group, Hickam Field, Hawaii, in what is known as the Farthing Report. Farthing completed the report on July 10, 1941. Its intent was to analyze the use of bombardment aviation as a defense for Hawaii. It also noted that "the early morning attack is, therefore, the best plan of action to the enemy."

Q. Who said, "I feel that a surprise attack [submarine, air or combined] on Pearl Harbor is a possibility"?

A. Admiral Husband E. Kimmel, Cincus, on February 18, 1941, in a letter to Admiral Harold R. Stark, CNO.

Q. Who said, "My Peruvian colleague told a member of my staff that he heard...that Japanese military forces planned...to attempt a surprise attack on Pearl Harbor"?

A. Considered one of the most remarkable dispatches ever sent by a U.S. diplomat, U.S. Ambassador to Japan Joseph C. Grew sent the above to the State Department within *a month after Admiral Yamamoto first disclosed to anyone* his bold plan for attacking Pearl Harbor in January 1941. However, it received only token interest in official circles, since Japanese fiction writers had used the theme of attacking Pearl Harbor for several years and the report was considered just an unfounded rumor based on such tales. Nonetheless, on February 1, 1941, the Office of Naval Intelligence paraphrased the ambassador's dispatch and forwarded it to Admiral Husband E. Kimmel in Hawaii.

FACT General Hein Ter Poorten, commander of the Netherlands East Indies Army, advised the U.S. military observer in Java, Brigadier General Elliott Thorpe, in early December 1941, that his intelligence staff had intercepted a Japanese code which stated that Japan would attack Hawaii, the Philippines, Malaya and Thailand shortly. He further noted that the signal for hostilities against the U.S. would be the message "East wind, rain." General Thorpe sent this information to Washington along with three others on the same subject, but Washington's reply requested he send no further information on the subject.

> **FACT** Captain Johan Ranneft, the Dutch naval attaché in Washington, was told on December 6, 1941, that two Japanese aircraft carriers were proceeding east between Japan and Hawaii. While at the Office of U.S. Naval Intelligence, he asked where the carriers were. An officer placed a finger on a wall chart and indicated a position between 300 and 400 miles northwest of Honolulu.

Q. Who said, "Do you mean to say that they [the Japanese fleet] could be rounding Diamond Head this minute and you wouldn't know?"

A. Admiral Husband E. Kimmel to his intelligence officer on Oahu on December 2, 1941, five days before the infamous attack, when the officer informed Kimmel that the Japanese carrier force that left its home waters in late November was still "missing" to U.S. plotters.

Q. Who said, "My impression of the Hawaiian [Pearl Harbor] problem has been that if no serious harm is done us during the *first six hours* of known hostilities, thereafter the existing defenses would discourage an enemy against the hazard of an attack"?

A. U.S. Army Chief of Staff George C. Marshall, who never considered that Japan could inflict the kind of harm he feared in the *first six minutes* (author's italics).

Q. Who said, "No, thanks, Betty, I feel I can get it through quickly enough," to whom concerning the final warning message to Pearl Harbor the morning of December 7?

A. General George Marshall in a telephone call to Admiral Harold R. (Betty) Stark. Marshall marked the message "First Priority — Secret," and it was sent by Western Union rather than through the U.S. Navy's rapid transmission system that Stark had offered. The message was "The Japanese are presenting at 1 P.M. Eastern Standard Time today what amounts to an ultimatum. Also they are under orders to destroy their code machine immediately. Just what significance the hour set may have we do not know, but be on the alert accordingly." It arrived on Oahu at the Western Union office and was delivered some time after the attack began. It was not completely decoded until seven hours after the attack had begun, and only then did General Short and Admiral Kimmel receive copies of it.

Q. Who said, "An attack upon these [Hawaiian] islands is not impossible and in certain situations it might not be improbable"?

A. Lieutenant General Walter C. Short, the U.S. Army commander in Hawaii, in an address at the University of Hawaii on August 12, 1941.

Q. Who said, "If I were in charge in Washington I would relieve Kimmel at once. It doesn't make any difference why a man fails in the Navy, he has failed"?

A. Admiral Husband E. Kimmel, speaking about himself and his expected fate, to two staff members after the Pearl Harbor attack.

Q. To whom was the following said in Moscow by a Japanese newsman on December 7: "So sorry, we sank your fleet this morning. Supposing we are at war"?

A. To American newsman C. L. Sulzberger at the Grand Hotel in Moscow.

Q. Who said: "Today all of us are in the same boat with you and the people of the Empire and it is a ship which will not and cannot be sunk"?

A. President Franklin D. Roosevelt to Prime Minister Winston S. Churchill on December 8, 1941, shortly after Congress declared war on Japan.

Q. Who asked FDR, "How did they catch us with our pants down, Mr. President?" upon hearing details of the Pearl Harbor attack on December 7?

A. Senator Thomas Connally (Democrat of Texas) on the evening of the attack when Cabinet and congressional leaders met with FDR.

FACT After Pearl Harbor, critics repeatedly asked why the U.S. fleet was in port rather than out at sea. The simple answer was a critical fuel shortage. Admiral Kimmel wanted to keep two task forces at sea at all times while only one remained in port at a time. However, all fuel for the fleet had to be brought to Hawaii from the U.S. mainland, and only four of the Pacific fleet's tankers were capable of fueling ships at sea. As an example of fuel consumption, it is noted that a single destroyer at sea was capable of consuming its entire fuel supply in thirty hours.

Messages and Quotations

Q. "A lot of Moxey" (earlier spelled "Moxie" when it was attributed to a soft drink), referred to whom or what?

A. RAF Squadron Leader E. L. Moxey, the designer of a disarming device for bombs, was regarded as an exceptionally courageous individual for his dangerous work.

Q. "Dear Kitty:" Who began each writing with that salutation?

A. Anne Frank, who began entries in her diary that way. The house she and her family hid in for two years is in Amsterdam, Holland. Open to the public, it remains exactly as it was on the day they were arrested in 1944.

Q. Who said, "Before we're through with 'em, the Japanese language will be spoken only in hell"?

A. U.S. Rear Admiral William F. Halsey, from the bridge of the aircraft carrier USS *Enterprise* (CV-6) as he returned to Pearl Harbor and saw the destruction of the U.S. fleet.

Q. Who said, "This is not the end. It is not even the beginning of the end. But it is, perhaps, the end of the beginning"?

A. British Prime Minister Winston S. Churchill as he referred to the British victory over Rommel at El Alamein during a November 10, 1942, speech.

Q. Who is credited with coining the phrase the "United Nations"?

A. President Franklin D. Roosevelt.

Q. Who said; "I have...a reactionary Army and a Christian Navy"?
A. Adolf Hitler, whose description of the three branches of the Wehrmacht began, "I have a National Socialist Air Force, a reactionary..."

Q. Who said, "Guts, as well as guns, win battles"?
A. U.S. Admiral Harold R. Stark.

Q. Who said, "The highest obligation and privilege of citizenship is that of bearing arms for one's country"?
A. U.S. General George S. Patton.

Q. Who said, "Send us more Japs"?
A. While Wake Island was under a fierce attack by the Japanese in December 1941, the U.S. Navy began assembling a relief expedition from Pearl Harbor, but the plan was soon abandoned because of the admitted weakened condition of U.S. forces at Pearl. As a result, Pearl Harbor sent a radio message to the U.S. Marines on Wake. "Is there anything we can provide?" it asked. The leathernecks' reply was "Send us more Japs."

Q. Who said, "No one doubts that the British and American naval forces now in the Far East could easily destroy the Japanese Navy"?
A. The *Atlanta Constitution*, on September 20, 1941. It was typical of optimistic remarks that appeared in many newspapers across the country, which did not consider Japan a strong potential enemy.

Q. Who said, "If there were ever men and a fleet ready for any emergency it's Uncle Sam's fighting ships"?
A. The *Honolulu Advertiser*, on February 1, 1941, less than a month after Japanese Admiral Yamamoto first discussed the idea of attacking the U.S. fleet at Pearl Harbor.

FACT U.S. General Douglas MacArthur took maximum advantage of his famous "I shall return" utterance upon leaving the Philippines. He had cigarettes and candy bars imprinted with the initials I.S.R. (I Shall Return) and sent to the islands by submarines during the Japanese occupation.

Q. What was the historic battle cry in the streets of Paris that signified the insurrection against German occupation in August 1944?

A. *Aux barricades!* Here a French woman, wearing a German helmet on her head and the Croix de Lorraine armband, prepares for the battle near the Prefecture of Police.

Roughol Photo

Q. Who said, "It now turns out that Japan was one of our customers who wasn't right"?

A. In a play on words (the customer is *always* right) the *Arkansas Gazette* made the comment after the Japanese attack on Pearl Harbor.

Q. Who said, "He's a hero! Already he has massacred seven microphones, and he's still going..." about General Charles de Gaulle and his radio broadcasts urging Frenchmen to join the Free French?

A. The Roman daily newspaper *Il Travaso*.

Q. Who said, "You can get a man down quicker by hitting on the same tooth than by hitting him all over"?

A. U.S. Admiral Forest Sherman.

Q. Who said, "All the Axis is hearing the tolling of the bells, and we are doing the rope pulling"?

    a. Admiral William F. Halsey, Jr.

    b. Prime Minister Winston S. Churchill

    c. President Franklin D. Roosevelt

A. Admiral Halsey.

Q. Who said, "Don't tell me it can't be done...go out there and do it"?

A. U.S. General Lucian K. Truscott.

Q. Who said, "To defeat the enemy, come to grips with him and fight him"?

    a. Field Marshal Erwin Rommel

    b. General George S. Patton

    c. Admiral Chester Nimitz

    d. General Omar N. Bradley

A. Admiral Chester Nimitz.

Q. Who said, "The chief impression you get from watching the German Army at work...is a gigantic, impersonal war machine, run as coolly and efficiently as our automobile industry in Detroit"?

A. American journalist William L. Shirer, who covered the early stages of the war from Germany. After the war, Shirer wrote *The Rise and Fall of The Third Reich*.

Q. About whom did U.S. General Mark Clark say, "A more gallant
   fighting organization never existed"?
      a. British commandos
      b. American airborne troops
      c. French Expeditionary Corps
      d. Italian marines
A. The Expeditionary Corps, made up of Moroccans, Algerians and
   French Nationals, formed by French General Alphonse Juin in North
   Africa.

U.S. Army Photo

Q. Who said, "There is no one more frustrated than a newspaperman with a story he can't get out"?

A. General Mark Clark, commander of the U.S. Fifth Army at the final briefing before the invasion of Italy. He expected that facilities would be arranged for the press shortly after the "quick victory."

Q. Who said, "Stand fast! We're staying here. Marines don't retreat"?

A. Lieutenant Robert Glenn, USMC, on Iwo Jima.

Q. Who said, "Aim not only to hit first, but to keep hitting, and oftener than the other fellow"?

A. U.S. Admiral Ernest J. King

Q. Who said, "I shall send in my resignation as an Italian if anyone objects to our fighting the Greeks"?

A. Benito Mussolini to Count Ciano when questioned whether the Duce had discussed the attack on Greece with Marshal Badoglio.

Q. Who said, "It is criminal to take part in a war which, disguised as a war for the preservation of democracy, is nothing but a war for the destruction of National Socialism"?
> a. U.S. pacifist Father Conlon
> b. Soviet diplomat V. I. Molotov
> c. Deputy Fuehrer Rudolf Hess

A. Molotov, underscoring the "joint fight of Germany and the Soviet Union against the capitalist powers of the West," on October 31, 1939.

Q. Who said, "We will win only by fighting"?
> a. Dwight D. Eisenhower
> b. Chester Nimitz
> c. Winston Churchill

A. U.S. Admiral Chester Nimitz.

Q. Who said "I'm an officer of the Fifth Army Headquarters. I guess I can play, can't I?" to a group of officers and enlisted man having a game of softball in Morocco?

A. General Mark Clark, who landed his Piper Cub on a field where the game was in progress. He managed to play at first base.

FACT Swiss-German actor Emil Jannings, who won the first-ever Academy Award for Best Actor (1927–28) for his work in *The Last Command* and *The Way of All Flesh*, made propaganda films for Germany during the war.

Q. Who said, "I shall do as Bertoldo did. He accepted the death sentence on the condition that he could choose the tree on which he was to be hanged. Needless to say, he never found that tree"?

A. Italian dictator Benito Mussolini to Count Galeazzo Ciano in explaining how he would agree to enter the war but reserve for himself the choice of the moment. The conversation took place on April 2, 1940.

Q. Who said, "Cease firing, but if any enemy planes appear, shoot 'em down in a friendly fashion"?

A. U.S. Admiral William F. Halsey, Jr., in August 1945, after Japan announced it had accepted the Allied terms for surrender.

Q. Who said, "[It was] a submarine without a periscope" in describing the headquarters of French General Gamelin in 1940?

A. French General Charles de Gaulle. The remark referred to Gamelin's failure to have adequate radio contact with his army in the field.

Q. Who said, "We shall never forget that it was our submarines that held the lines against the enemy while our fleets replaced losses and repaired wounds"?

A. U.S. Admiral Chester W. Nimitz.

Q. Who said, "A serious day, rich in crises. It seems that we are in trouble"?

A. German Field Marshal Fedor von Bock, in his diary on June 6, 1940, commenting on the unexpected resistance his troops were receiving from the French. The quote could also have been used four years to the day later as the Allies stormed the beaches at Normandy.

Q. What did the message "Execute Pontiam" signify to the troops on Corregidor in 1942?

A. Sent by General Jonathan Wainwright to all commands, it notified them of the surrender to the Japanese on May 6.

Q. Who said, "Three demoralizing factors, inactivity, propaganda and drink," were responsible for the rapid German victory over the French in 1940?

A. Colonel A. Goutard, in his book *The War of Lost Opportunities*, to describe the general state of mind of the twenty divisions France fielded in 1940.

Q. Who said, "Even if he is 4F he can feel like a hero," and about what?

A. New York department store Lord & Taylor, as part of its campaign to sell "Ike Jackets" to civilians. The jacket was a copy of the one first worn by General Dwight D. Eisenhower and created especially for him.

Q. Name the Rumanian dictator who said, "You can't even shoot straight!" as a firing squad's efforts to execute him failed on the first attempt?

A. Ion Antonescu. He had aligned himself with the Axis out of a violent hate of the Soviets. Not only did the first attempt to execute him fail, but a second one did as well. The commanding officer of the Soviet firing squad was required to give him the coup de grace.

Q. Who wrote the following to one of Britain's leading advocates of tank warfare: "To Captain B. H. Liddell Hart from one of his disciples in tank affairs"?

A. Germany's foremost tank warfare strategist General Heinz Guderian. The inscription appears on a photograph Guderian gave Hart prior to the outbreak of war. Hart also received a similar tribute from German General Hasso von Manteuffel.

FACT The 1942 movie *Mrs. Miniver* had a tremendous effect on American public opinion and is considered to have been of great value in increasing the empathy of Americans for the British. It portrayed the quiet heroism of entire families, housewives, the middle class and the wealthy. It included scenes of the evacuation of Dunkirk and generally depicted the British in the stereotypes many Americans held. President Franklin D. Roosevelt was so touched by the closing monologue that he had it printed on leaflets and dropped over occupied Europe. The film premiered on June 4, 1942, two years to the day that Winston Churchill had made his Fight on the Beaches speech.

FACT There is a three-foot marble monument dedicated to a duck in the city park in Freiburg, Germany. The duck reportedly warned the townspeople of approaching Allied aircraft, often before the normal alarm system, and as a result many lives were saved. In November 1944, the dependable duck squawked its final alarm but became a casualty of the air raid that followed. On the ninth anniversary of the raid the monument was unveiled with the following inscription: "God's creature laments, accuses and reminds!"

Q. Who said, "When outstanding heroism was required, it was commonplace among the boarding party"?

A. U.S. Admiral Daniel V. Gallery, reporting on the capture of U-505 by the USS *Guadalcanal*.

Q. Who said, "We all admire a ship that can't be licked"?
      a. Admiral Yamamoto
      b. Admiral Nimitz
      c. Admiral Doenitz

A. U.S. Admiral Chester Nimitz.

Q. Who said, "Perhaps I could be called a traitor, but that would not be facing reality. I believe I am a better German than those who follow Hitler. My goal, my duty, is to free Germany and the whole world from this scourge"?

A. Colonel Hans Oster, an aide to Admiral Wilhelm Canaris in the Abwehr. He made the statement to a Dutch major to whom he had passed vital information concerning Germany's ambitions in Holland. Oster provided a considerable amount of intelligence to neutrals during his tenure.

Q. Who said, "It looks like the real thing this time. The swine has left for the front"?
      a. German Colonel Hans Oster
      b. British Prime Minister Winston S. Churchill
      c. General Charles de Gaulle
      d. Soviet Premier Josef Stalin

A. Oster, the German Abwehr officer who passed on intelligence to the Allies. This message was given to Dutch military attache Major Sas at 10 P.M. on May 9, the night before the German attack on Belgium.

Q. Who said, "Hit 'em where they ain't"?
A. Though it is doubtful that the very proper General Douglas MacArthur would have phrased it that way, the remark sums up his tactics of assaulting Japanese islands.

Q. Who said, "There is nothing so unpleasant as partisan warfare. It is perhaps very important not to make reprisals on hostages at the first outbreak of partisan warfare"?
A. German Field Marshal Erwin Rommel. The quote appears as an entry in his diary of September 2, 1942. In 1944, Rommel protested to Hitler about the massacre of French civilians at Oradour-sur-Glane by the SS Das Reich Panzer Division and demanded exemplary punishment for those responsible. Hitler's response was a violent rebuff.

Q. Who said, "I have no intention of carrying out that order," referring to any possible order that would require France to turn her fleet over to Germany after the armistice.
A. French Admiral Jean François Darlan, in a letter to Vice Admiral Le Luc on May 28, 1940. If the order ever came, he said, he wanted all able ships to put to sea and make for the nearest British port.

Q. Who said, "Everything that flies is my concern"?
A. The commander of the Luftwaffe, Hermann Goering.

Q. Who said, "He who tortures animals wounds the feelings of the German people"?
A. The author may have been Reichsmarschall Hermann Goering, in whose office the legend hung.

FACT The 12,000-acre Bialowieza National Park in Poland is the result of conservation efforts undertaken by German Reichsmarschall Hermann Goering. As Master of the German Forests (one of many titles), he took steps to ensure that the devastation the area received at the hands of German troops was reversed. Goering had the forest restocked with animals and put a strict limit on hunting. The park is considered the largest remaining area of the primeval forest that once covered much of Europe.

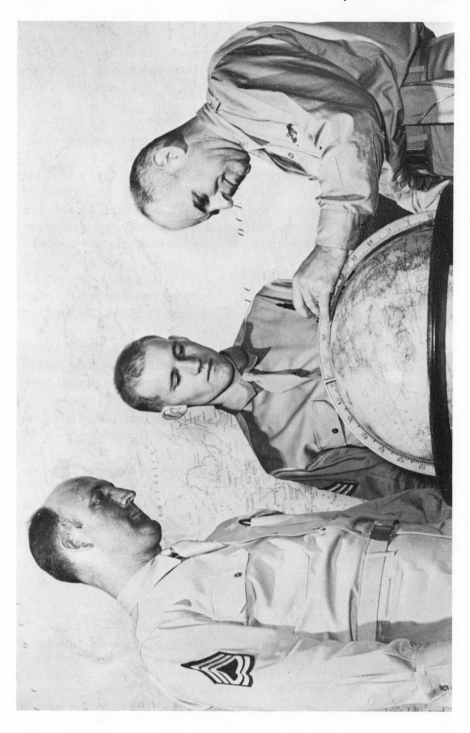

> **FACT** By August 1940, Britain's Home Guard contained one million volunteers. However, it was nearly impossible to arm them. Guns, swords and ammunition were taken from military museums and war memorials, and unlikely sources such as the Drury Lane Theatre contributed a dozen old, rusty rifles. The task of arming the Home Guard was so difficult for a time that cutlasses from the days of Admiral Nelson were actually given out.

Q. Who said, "I don't think much of the name 'Local Defense Volunteers,' I think 'Home Guard' would be better"?

A. Prime Minister Winston S. Churchill, who continued: "Don't hesitate to change on account of having already made armlets, etc., if it is thought the title of Home Guard would be more compulsive."

Q. Who said, "Appallingly shameful; appallingly stupid" in reference to the British attack on the French fleet in Mers el-Kebir?

A. British Admiral of the Fleet Sir John H. D. Cunningham, in 1962. In 1940, Admiral Cunningham was faced with a similar prospect when he received orders to eliminate the French ships (Force X) in the eastern Mediterranean. Instead he worked out a demobilizing program with French Admiral Godfroy that removed the ships as a possible threat without the loss of lives.

Q. Who called the years between the two world wars "that period of exhaustion which has been described as peace"?

A. British Prime Minister Winston S. Churchill.

Q. Who said, "Fighter planes win battles, but photo reconnaissance wins wars"?

A. U.S. General Hap Arnold.

Q. Who said, "They flew from Shangri-La," when asked where the planes that participated in the Doolittle raid came from?

A. President Franklin D. Roosevelt, in an effort to protect the identity and position of the aircraft carrier USS *Hornet* (CV-8). By the time Jimmy Doolittle and two of the men who participated in the raid, Sergeant Eldred V. Scott (left) and Sergeant David J. Thatcher, got together for this 1942 photo, the Army Air Force flying legend was Brigadier General James H. Doolittle.

U.S. Army Photo

Q. Who said, "Anything new, Georges"?

A. Amédée Bussière, prefect of the Paris Police Department, to his valet on the morning of August 19, 1944, upon awakening. The reply was "Yes...they have come back." The "they" was the police force, which had been on strike. That morning they gathered to capture the Prefecture of Police building, the central point in the insurrection to liberate Paris. In photo above, a policeman and other members of the Free French Forces of the Interior, attempting to get to the Prefecture later in the day, meet German opposition at Pont Neuf, one of the bridges that cross the Seine.

U.S. Army Photo

FACT Dusko Popov, a German spy whom the British compromised and turned into a double agent, was chased out of the U.S. by J. Edgar Hoover, who said, "I can catch spies without you or anybody else's help." The Germans had sent Popov to the U.S. in August 1941 to get information about Pearl Harbor for the Japanese. Popov told the British, who in turn told the U.S., but Hoover was not interested and sent the double agent packing.

Q. Who said, "It appears the peacock will be on time"?

A. U.S. Admiral William F. Halsey, Jr., authorizing U.S. P-38 aircraft to intercept and shoot down the aircraft carrying Japanese Admiral Isoroku Yamamoto in April 1943. The last part read, "Fan his tail."

Q. Who said, "The issue is in doubt"?

A. USMC Major James Devereaux. It was the last message sent from Wake Island before it was overrun by the Japanese.

Q. Who said, "The second best air force was no more use than the second best hand at poker"?

A. U.S. General Henry Harley Arnold.

Q. Who said, "Sighted sub, sank same"?
   a. Lieutenant Commander Robert Dixon
   b. Captain Fred M. Smith
   c. Lieutenant Donald F. Mason

A. Dixon reported sinking the Japanese aircraft carrier *Shoho* with "Scratch one flattop." Smith, flying a P-38, radioed "Saw steamer, strafed same, sank same, some sight, signed Smith." Mason, in a Lockheed Hudson in March 1942, reported "Sighted sub, sank same."

Q. Who said, "Just sight, track, shoot and sink"?

A. Commander Dudley W. Morton of the submarine USS *Wahoo* (SS-238).

Q. Who said, "Expended four torpedoes and one Jap destroyer"?

A. U.S. Navy Commander Sam Dealy, upon reporting the sinking of the *Ikazuki* by the submarine USS *Harder*.

Appendix

Ships have always held a fascination for sailors and non-sailors alike. Enshrined warships from past conflicts going as far back as the American Revolution have, over the decades, remained to fascinate anew each generation that views them. It is therefore not surprising that fighting ships from World War II that have been maintained as memorials draw increasing numbers of visitors each year.

Battlefield memorials mark the very earth where this nation first won its independence and then more than four score years later preserved it. Bunker Hill, Yorktown, Saratoga, Lexington, Bull Run and Gettysburg are but a representative few. Yet it is impossible to mark locations on the high seas where our nation's fate so often hung in the balance.

So we've done the next best thing. We've preserved the ships. Not all of them, to be sure, and probably far too few. As you move through the pages of this section it is worth reflecting for a moment that these World War II warships have been saved from being recycled as scrap in almost all cases by what began as the dedicated and determined efforts of small groups of people.

We've culled the records of memorials, commissions and commemorative displays and hope we have compiled as complete a list of U.S. World War II ships as exists anywhere.

But as we did this we couldn't help thinking about those great ships that were not so fortunate. The USS *Enterprise* (CV-6) and USS *Nevada* (BB-36) immediately come to mind. The former was sold for scrap and the latter ended up as a target ship for atomic bomb testing off Bikini atoll.

What follows is a listing of ships that are open to public view. The first thirteen are fairly complete and include photos. Beyond that we've condensed the information either in the interest of brevity or because of incomplete or insufficient information.

USS *Alabama* (BB-60) and USS *Drum* (SS-228)

Located at Battleship Alabama Memorial Park, Battleship Parkway, Mobile, Alabama. Open to visitors 8 A.M. until sunset every day of the year except Christmas. Parking is one dollar and admission for persons twelve years or older is $3.50; under twelve years, $1.50; under six years old there is no charge. Group rates available for ten or more. Armed forces personnel admitted free. Tours are not conducted. Visitors receive printed numbered tour guides which correspond to numbered arrows on the two ships. The site also includes a P-51 Mustang, a gull-winged Corsair and other aircraft and historic ships. Approximately 300,000 people visit the memorial annually. The single admission covers all memorial attractions and there is a gift shop on the premises.

The 35,000-ton USS *Alabama* is a sister ship to the USS *Massachusetts*, USS *Indiana* and USS *South Dakota*. She was launched at the Norfolk Naval Shipyard, Portsmouth, Virginia, on February 16, 1942, while General Douglas MacArthur's troops were fighting on Bataan. She eventually won nine battle stars in World War II for action in the Gilberts, Marshalls, Pacific raids, Hollandia, Marianas, Western Carolines, Leyte, Okinawa and Japan.

The submarine USS *Drum* was launched on May 12, 1941, and earned twelve battle stars on thirteen war patrols and is credited with sinking fifteen enemy ships for a total of 80,580 tons of shipping. She sank the Japanese seaplane tender *Mizuho* and three cargo ships on her first patrol between April 14 and June 12, 1942.

USS *Arizona* (BB-39)

Located exactly where it was on December 7, 1941, Battleship Row, Ford Island, Pearl Harbor, Oahu, Hawaii. The USS *Arizona* Memorial spans the sunken hull of the battleship which is resting in thirty-eight feet of water. The U.S. Navy conducts daily free tours on a first-come, first-served basis, which also include a documentary film about the Japanese attack. At present there are also four civilian tour boats making daily tours for a nominal fee, but they do not debark passengers at the memorial itself, something the Navy tour does. Navy tour passengers can visit the three sections of the memorial: the museum room, which houses mementos of the ship; the assembly area, capable of accommodating 200 persons for ceremonies; and the shrine room, where names of the 1,177 U.S. personnel killed on the ship are engraved on a marble wall. The civilian boats tour the harbor and play tapes that explain the action on the morning of the attack and pause alongside the memorial for a moment of silence. Well over one million people visit the USS *Arizona* Memorial annually. It is the most popular tourist attraction in Hawaii.

The USS *Arizona* was launched at the New York Navy Yard on June 19, 1915, and commissioned on October 17, 1916. She was a member of the honor escort that brought President Woodrow Wilson to France for the 1918 Paris Peace Conference. Throughout the 1920s she was the mightiest ship of the U.S. fleet and was modernized between the wars. On April 2, 1940, she was assigned to duty at Pearl Harbor. She left the U.S. west coast for the last time in 1941, reaching Pearl Harbor on July 8, 1941.

The ship is no longer in commission, but in memory of the men who lost their lives on the "Day that will live in infamy" the Navy has granted special permission for the American flag to fly over the USS *Arizona*.

USS *Becuna* (SS-319) and USS *Olympia*

Located at Penn's Landing, Delaware Avenue and Spruce Street, Philadelphia, Pennsylvania. Open to visitors from 10 A.M. to 4:30 P.M. seven days a week except Christmas and New Year's Day. Summer hours are extended until 6 P.M. Admission is $2.50 for adults and $1.25 for children under twelve years of age. Information on group rates available. Purchases made in the ship's store help to preserve these two historic ships. One particularly interesting item is souvenir coins made from the *Olympia*'s propellers, priced at $7.50 each.

Though the senior attraction here is the USS *Olympia* we begin this listing with the World War II submarine USS *Becuna*, a guppy-class boat that was commissioned on May 27, 1944. She served as the submarine flagship of the Southwest Pacific Fleet under General Douglas MacArthur. The *Becuna* earned four battle stars in five war patrols and also received a Presidential Unit Citation. After a postwar refit, she continued to see active duty in the Atlantic and Mediterranean during the Korean and Vietnam wars. She was decommissioned on October 1, 1969. The *Becuna* is the last of her type open for public exhibit.

Naval buffs and military historians need little introduction to the USS *Olympia*. Launched on November 5, 1892, and retired on September 1, 1922, she played a part in all the major American actions that marked this country as a world power.

Commodore Dewey stood on her bridge on May 1, 1898, found himself eyeball-to-eyeball with the Spanish fleet off the Philippine Islands and uttered the historic "You may fire when you are ready, Gridley," thus exploding the Battle of Manila Bay into history. Her log includes delivering the peace-keeping force to Murmansk, Russia, in 1918, service as flagship for U.S. Navy ships in the eastern Mediterranean, flagship for the North Atlantic Squadron and service as a training ship for Annapolis midshipmen.

USS *Bowfin* (SS-287)

Located at 11 Arizona Memorial Drive, Honolulu, Hawaii. Open to visitors every day 9:30 A.M. to 4:30 P.M. Adult admission is three dollars and children between six and twelve years can board the boat for a dollar. Children under six years of age are not permitted aboard the *Bowfin*. No federal or state funds are used for the maintenance. The exhibit is operated by the Pacific Fleet Submarine Memorial Association as a memorial to the fifty-two U.S. submarines and 3,505 submariners of World War II who are considered "still on patrol." Visitors are provided with lightweight radio wands which receive transcribed narratives at stations throughout the submarine. Additionally, tour guides are in the boat to answer questions. The gift shop offers fairly priced items and the volunteer staff is pleasant.

The USS *Bowfin* was launched at Portsmouth, New Hampshire, on December 7, 1942, the first anniversary of the Pearl Harbor attack. She was commissioned on May 1, 1943. During her nine war patrols between August 1943 and August 1945, the USS *Bowfin* sank 179,946 tons of enemy shipping (forty-four ships), and one of her commanders, Walter T. Griffith, ranks as the seventh-highest-scoring American submarine commander in the war (he is credited with seventeen ships while serving on the *Bowfin* and USS *Bullhead*). The USS *Bowfin* earned eight battle stars and both the Presidential Unit Citation and the Navy Unit Commendation.

The USS *Bowfin* saw a variety of assignments after World War II and was finally decommissioned in December 1971. Rather than see this fierce fighting boat sold for scrap and possibly end up being recycled into razor blades, a small group in Hawaii formed the association that persuaded the U.S. Navy to give them the boat, and the result is this exhibit.

USS *Croaker* (SS-246)

Located at the Fort Griswold Moorings, 359 Thames Street, Groton, Connecticut. Open to visitors from April 15 to October 15 from 9 A.M. to 5 P.M. with the last tour starting at 4:30 P.M. From October 16 to April 14, it is open from 9 A.M. but closes at 3 P.M. That is also the hour of the last tour. Adults pay three dollars admission; children from five to eleven pay $1.50; children under five may board free with an adult. Military personnel in uniform are admitted free. There are group rates for ten or more, pre-scheduled, arriving together. The guided tour takes approximately one half hour. The exhibit has a snack bar–restaurant and gift shop.

The USS *Croaker* was commissioned at the U.S. Naval Submarine Base, Groton, Connecticut, on April 21, 1944. She participated in six war patrols in the Pacific and is credited with sinking a Japanese cruiser, four tankers, two freighters, two escort craft, a minesweeper and an ammunition ship.

After World War II the *Croaker* returned to Connecticut and participated as an active member of the fleet until she was stricken from the record in 1971. She is maintained by the Submarine Memorial Association, Incorporated, which is also involved in obtaining the world's first nuclear-powered submarine, the USS *Nautilus*, as a permanent national monument exhibit near the USS *Croaker*. Information about this effort is available from the association. (The *Nautilus* was built at the nearby Electric Boat Division of General Dynamics.)

USS *Intrepid* (CV-11)

Located at Pier 86 on West 46th Street in New York City. The Intrepid
Sea-Air-Space Museum offers considerably more than an exciting visit
to one of the only two U.S. World War II aircraft carriers open to visitors,
since it combines exhibits that feature other areas of interest noted
in its name. From June 1 to September 30, it is open from 10 A.M. until 8 P.M. and between October 1 and May 31, it closes one hour earlier.
However, the ticket office closes at 6 P.M. and 5 P.M., respectively. Adult
admission is five dollars, children $2.50, senior citizens four dollars and
groups of ten or more are four dollars for adults, and two dollars for
those eighteen and younger.

Built in 1943 in Newport News, Virginia, at a cost of $44 million,
the *Intrepid* carried 360 officers and 3,008 enlisted men during wartime service. She was nicknamed the Fighting I but because she was
the most frequently hit U.S. ship in the war she became known as the
Evil I. Her combat record would easily fill several pages. Planes from
her decks sank the two largest battleships (72,809 tons) ever built, the
Yamato and *Musashi*. In the 1960s she was the prime recovery ship
during two Mercury and Gemini space missions.

The museum section of the exhibit (on the hangar deck) features four
theme halls: the United States Navy Hall uses special effects to recreate
the excitement of carrier aviation and puts an emphasis on the modern
peacekeeping Navy; Intrepid Hall takes visitors back to the action of
World War II; Pioneer Hall details man's early probes into the sky with
flight; Technologies Hall covers the great advances in sea, air and space
that have had a profound influence on the twentieth century. The Flight
Deck includes many historic aircraft. The Intrepid Sea-Air-Space
Museum opened to the public in the summer of 1982, and new exhibits
are being added regularly.

USS *Kidd* (DD-661)

Located in Baton Rouge, Louisiana. Opened daily to the public for the first time in June 1983. Admission for adults is three dollars for touring the *Kidd*, but there will be no charge for admission to a proposed $2.5 million museum facility being built near the ship. The museum currently has an exhibit on display at the Louisiana Arts and Sciences Center, also at this location. The Louisiana Naval War Memorial Commission expects that a good number of the 200,000 annual visitors to the Arts and Sciences Center will also visit the USS *Kidd* and the museum. A gift shop and snack bar are planned for the complex.

Commissioned in April 1943, the *Kidd* saw heavy action in World War II. She was involved in every major naval campaign in the Pacific and earned four battle stars. Engagements she was involved in included Okinawa, Leyte, the Gilberts, Marshalls and the Philippines. Her nickname is the Pirate of the Pacific. She earned four more battle stars for her service during the Korean War.

The USS *Kidd* was decommissioned in 1964 and became part of the Atlantic Reserve Fleet until 1982, when ownership was transferred to the Louisiana Naval War Memorial Commission. Accompanying photo was taken during her days of active service.

USS *Ling* (SS-297)

Located in Borg Park on the Hackensack River at the intersection of Court and River Streets, Hackensack, New Jersey. Admission for adults is two dollars, for children twelve and under it is one dollar. A discount of 25 percent is offered to groups of fifteen and up. Tours are conducted seven days a week from June to September from 10:15 A.M. on, with the last tour starting at 5 P.M. Between October and May the last tour goes off at 4 P.M. There is a gift shop and exhibit of nautical items of interest. Money raised through the boat tours and the gift shop is used by the non-profit Submarine Memorial Association to maintain the exhibits, which, besides the USS *Ling*, include several missiles, torpedoes, mines and anchors. The boat is heated for winter touring.

The USS *Ling* was commissioned on June 8, 1945, and managed to get in one Atlantic war patrol before the war ended. She is the last of the fleet-type submarines that patrolled American shores in the war years and was built by the Cramp Shipbuilding Company and outfitted at the Boston Navy Yard. She was decommissioned on October 26, 1946, and became part of the New London Group, Atlantic Reserve Fleet, until she was reactivated as a Submarine Naval Reserve training vessel in 1960.

In December 1962, the *Ling* was converted from an SS to an AGSS submarine and served as one of the most elaborate and authentic training aids in the world. She was decommissioned for a second, and final, time in December 1971. She arrived in Hackensack at her present berth on January 13, 1973.

While on active service, she carried a complement of ninety-five officers and men and an armament capacity of twenty-four torpedoes.

USS *Massachusetts* (BB-59)

Located at Battleship Cove, Fall River, Massachusetts, at Exit 5, I-95. The battleship is the main attraction of an exhibit that includes five other ships and a marine museum. All six attractions are open throughout the year except Thanksgiving and Christmas, from 9 A.M. to 5 P.M. and until 8 P.M. between June 30 and Labor Day. Admission is $4.50 for adults, $2.50 for children six to thirteen, and tots two to five get in for seventy-five cents. Group rates are available upon request.

The museum contains 131 beautifully executed ship models ranging in size from a half inch to twelve feet long. At several locations visitors can press a button and hear background information about the particular exhibit being viewed.

The other ships at Battleship Cove include the destroyer USS *Joseph P. Kennedy* (DD-850); the submarine USS *Lionfish* (SS-298); a PT boat; the gunboat *Asheville*; and the bow of the cruiser USS *Fall River* (CA-131).

The USS *Massachusetts* holds the distinction of being the first battleship to fire 16-inch guns at the enemy in World War II, in the Atlantic, and the last to fire them, this time in the Pacific. From that first volley until the last, she traveled over 225,000 miles and participated in thirty-five battles. Her nickname is Big Mamie.

The USS *Massachusetts* is the official state memorial to those who gave their lives in all branches of the service during World War II. The memorial area contains the names of the more than 13,000 Bay State residents who died in the war. The destroyer USS *Joseph P. Kennedy* is the official state memorial to the more than 4,500 who died in the Korean and Vietnam conflicts.

USS *Missouri* (BB-63)

Located at the Puget Sound Naval Shipyard, Bremerton, Washington. Of all the ships in this section the battleship USS *Missouri* is the only one that is still the property of the U.S. Navy. She is preserved as part of the mothball fleet. There is no charge to board and visit her, and normal visiting hours from Memorial Day to Labor Day are 10 A.M. to 8 P.M. At other times hours are noon to 4 P.M. There is a refreshment stand at the site, and souvenirs are available.

We should note that if Congress approves funding for reactivation of this mighty battleship during 1983 it will join the USS *New Jersey* as part of the active fleet.

The USS *Missouri* was built at the New York Naval Shipyard and was launched on January 29, 1944. She was commissioned on June 11 of that year and remained in service until being decommissioned on February 26, 1955. She transited the Panama Canal and entered the western Pacific in January 1945.

The *Missouri* participated in operations against Okinawa, Iwo Jima and the Japanese mainland. It was on her decks, while in Tokyo Bay on September 2, 1945, that the instrument of surrender was signed by the representatives of the Japanese government, thus ending World War II.

Between 225,000 and 250,000 people visit the USS *Missouri* annually.

USS *North Carolina* (BB-55)

Located in Wilmington, North Carolina. The *North Carolina* is open every day of the year from 8 A.M. to 8 P.M. in the summer and closes at sunset during other times. Admission for those twelve and over is $2.50; children six to eleven, one dollar; and those five and under are free. A discount for groups of twenty or more is available when all tickets are purchased at once. A sound-and-light spectacular titled "The Immortal Showboat" (from her nickname) is presented nightly at 9 P.M. in the summer. It depicts her World War II record, replete with the majestic roar of the 16-inch guns. Admission for the show is $1.50 for adults; seventy-five cents for children six to eleven; and free for those five or under. Group discounts are available.

The USS *North Carolina* was the third U.S. Navy ship to bear that name. Her keel was laid at the Brooklyn Navy Yard on Navy Day, October 27, 1937, and she was launched on June 13, 1940. On April 9, 1941, she was commissioned. During her forty months in combat zones in World War II, the Showboat was reported sunk six times by Tokyo Rose.

She participated in the following Asiatic-Pacific campaigns: Guadalcanal and Tulagi; eastern Solomons; Gilbert Islands; Tarawa; Makin; Marshalls; Kwajalein; Roi; Namur; Guam; Saipan; Palau; Yap; Ulithi; Woleai; Satawan; Ponape; New Guinea; Aitape; Tanahmerah Bay; Humboldt Bay; Marianas; Tinian; Philippines; Iwo Jima; Honshu; Nansei; Shoto; Okinawa; Kerama-retto; Kyushu and the Inland Sea, among others.

The USS *North Carolina* Battleship Memorial is dedicated to the 10,000 state residents who died in World War II.

USS *Texas* (BB-35)

Located at Battleground Road, San Jacinto State Park, La Porte, Texas. Open to visitors from 10 A.M. to 5 P.M. every day of the year. Admission charges are three dollars for adults; two dollars for senior citizens; one dollar for those between six and eighteen. A gift shop is located aboard ship, and a snack bar is nearby as are several restaurants. Approximately 240,000 people visit the Grand Old Lady annually.

Commissioned in 1914 at Norfolk, Virginia, as a Dreadnought-class battleship, she saw action in both world wars. In World War II she made her combat debut in Operation Torch, the North African invasion, and participated in Operation Overlord, the D-Day invasion of Normandy. In the Pacific she made her presence felt at Iwo Jima and Okinawa. She is the third U.S. Navy ship named for the state of Texas. After the Japanese surrender, the USS *Texas* was one of the ships in the Magic Carpet Fleet that returned U.S. servicemen to the States.

Also enshrined at San Jacinto State Park along with the USS *Texas* is the USS *Cabrilla* (SS-288), a World War II submarine that sank 38,767 tons of enemy shipping during six of her eight war patrols.

Fleet Admiral Chester W. Nimitz was present at the dedication ceremonies when the USS *Texas* went on public display in 1948. The effort to preserve the *Texas* was the first such undertaking to create a ship-and-shore memorial to a state's naval namesake and encouraged other groups to create similar exhibits.

The San Jacinto State Park is a short drive by freeway from downtown Houston.

USS *Yorktown* (CV-10)

Located at Patriots Point, Charleston Harbor, South Carolina. the Fighting Lady is the main attraction at this exhibit that includes three other ships and several aircraft. Open daily to visitors from 9 A.M. to 6 P.M. (daylight saving time) and 9 A.M. to 5 P.M. (standard time). Admission is five dollars for adults; three dollars for children six to eleven; $4.50 for senior citizens and military personnel in uniform. Group rates are also available.

The ship's theater regularly shows the movie *The Fighting Lady*. There is a gift shop and restaurant.

The aircraft carrier USS *Yorktown* received the traditional champagne christening on April 15, 1943, at Newport News, Virginia. Mrs. Eleanor Roosevelt did the honors. Some ten months later the *Yorktown* celebrated the 7,000th landing on her decks. Her total landings in World War II alone were 31,170. The Fighting Lady earned fifteen battle stars during which time she was clearly the carrier to beat in the rivalries that always exist in any navy. She set records for the fastest launches and recoveries of aircraft and the heaviest flying schedules. She also set a record in shooting down 14½ enemy aircraft, while her planes accounted for 458 enemy planes in the air and 695 on the ground. She earned a presidential unit citation and several other awards. Truk, the Marianas, the Philippines, Iwo Jima, Okinawa, et al. — she was there.

Besides this great carrier, visitors can also see the destroyer USS *Laffey* (DD-724), hit by more Japanese kamikaze planes than any other ship in one battle; the World War II submarine USS *Clamagore* (SS-343); the world's first nuclear-powered merchant ship, the *Savannah*; plus aircraft, including a B-25 and eight others.

USS *Hazard* (AM-240)

Located at the Greater Omaha Marina, 2000 North 25th Street, East Omaha, Nebraska. Admission for adults is one dollar and children seventy-five-cents. Information on hours visitors may board is available by calling (402) 341-0550. In addition to the minesweeper USS *Hazard*, the Greater Omaha Marina also exhibits the post–World War II submarine USS *Marlin* (SST-2) and a McDonnell Douglas A-4 Skyhawk. There is a restaurant and lounge, golf-driving range, trailer campgrounds, three boat-launch ramps. The *Hazard* is the largest ship that has traveled this far inland, making the trek from Orange, Texas, to Omaha — a distance of 2,000 miles — in twenty-nine days. She now rests at the marina on the Missouri River.

The USS *Hazard* was launched on May 21, 1944, at Winslow, Washington, and commissioned on October 31, 1944. She screened convoys and swept mines at Eniwetok, the Philippines, Okinawa, Kerama-retto, the East China Sea, the Yellow Sea and Jinsen, Korea.

USS *Pampanito* (AG SS-383)

Located at Fisherman's Wharf in San Francisco, California. Admission is three dollars for adults; two dollars for juniors (twelve to eighteen) and seniors (over sixty-five); one dollar for children. She is open daily from 10 A.M. to 10 P.M.

The *Pampanito* was built at Portsmouth Naval Shipyard, New Hampshire, and was commissioned on November 6, 1943. She sank five enemy ships totaling 27,288 tons during her six war patrols. She rescued seventy-three Australian and British POW's after she and the USS *Sealion* sank two Japanese ships that were transporting them to labor camps.

FACT The American Battle Monuments Commission in Washington, D.C., administers U.S. Military cemeteries overseas. There are fourteen cemeteries on foreign soil where U.S. armed forces personnel killed in World War II are buried. The largest is near Manila, the Philippines, which has 17,208 graves and commemorates an additional 36,279 persons missing in action. The smallest is at Rhone, France, which has 861 graves and commemorates 293 missing personnel. A fifteenth cemetery, originally dedicated to personnel killed in the First World War at Suresnes, France, also has the graves of twenty-four unknown American dead from World War II.

Other Ships Open to Visitors

USS *Batfish* (AG SS-310), Muskogee, Oklahoma
USS *Cavalla* (AG SS-244), Galveston, Texas
USS *Cobia* (AG SS-245), Manitowoc, Wisconsin
USS *Codd* (SS-224), Cleveland, Ohio
USS *Inaugural* (AM-242), St. Louis, Missouri
PT 619, Memphis, Tennessee
USS *Little Rock* (CLG-4), Buffalo, New York
USS *Requin* (AG SS-481), Tampa, Florida
USS *Silversides* (SS-236), Chicago, Illinois
USS *Stewart* (DE-238), Galveston, Texas
USS *The Sullivans* (DDG-537), Buffalo, New York
USS *Torsk* (AS SS-423), Baltimore, Maryland
USS *Utah* (BB-31), Pearl Harbor, Oahu, Hawaii
U-505 (captured German submarine), Chicago, Illinois

Comparative German and American Officer Ranks

U.S. Army	Wehrmacht	SS (Schutz Staffeln)
General of the Army	Generalfeldmarschall	SS Reichsfuehrer
General	Generaloberst	Oberstgruppenfuehrer
Lieutenant General	General	Obergruppenfuehrer
Major General	Generalleutnant	Gruppenfuehrer
Brigadier General	Generalmajor	Brigadefuehrer
———	———	Oberfuehrer
Colonel	Oberst	Standartenfuehrer
Lieutenant Colonel	Oberstleutnant	Obersturmbannfuehrer
Major	Major	Sturmbannfuehrer
Captain	Hauptmann .	Hauptsturmfuehrer
First Lieutenant	Oberleutnant	Obersturmfuehrer
Second Lieutenant	Leutnant	Untersturmfuehrer
Warrant Officer	Unteroffizer	Hauptscharfuehrer

──────────────The McAuliffe Christmas Card──────────────

"Merry Christmas" from General Anthony C. McAuliffe

The 101st Airborne Division was totally surrounded by German units on Christmas Eve 1944 in Bastogne. McAuliffe's famous reply to the German surrender ultimatum ranks among the great quotes of that or any other war for its stunning simplicity. However, McAuliffe was not quite so abrupt with his own men when he circulated a mimeographed "greeting card" that December 24. Included in the text was the surrender ultimatum which the Germans typed on a captured American typewriter. Reprinted below, sans official letterhead, is General McAuliffe's Christmas message:

HEADQUARTERS 101ST AIRBORNE DIVISION
Office of the Division Commander

24 December 1944

What's Merry about all this, you ask? We're fighting — it's cold, we aren't home. All true but what has the proud Eagle Division accomplished with its worthy comrades of the 10th Armored Division, the 705th Tank Destroyer Battalion and all the rest? Just this: We have stopped cold everything that has been thrown at us from the North, East, South and West. We have identifications from four German Panzer Divisions, two German Infantry Divisions and one German Parachute Division. These units, spearheading the last desperate German lunge, were headed straight west for key points when the Eagle Division was hurriedly ordered to stem the advance. How effectively this was done will be written in history; not alone in our Division's glorious history but in World history. The Germans actually did surround us, their radios blared our doom. Their Commander demanded our surrender in the following impudent arrogance.

FACT The U.S. sustained a greater number of casualties during the Battle of the Bulge than U.S. forces under General MacArthur sustained throughout the entire war.

December 22nd 1944

"To the U.S.A. Commander of the encircled town of Bastogne.

"The fortune of war is changing. This time the U.S.A. forces in and near Bastogne have been encircled by strong German armored units. More German armored units have crossed the river Ourthe near Ortheuville, have taken Marche and reached St. Hubert by passing through Hombres-Sibret-Tillet. Libramont is in German hands.

"There is only one possibility to save the encircled U.S.A. Troop from total annihilation: that is the honorable surrender of the encircled town. In order to think it over, a term of two hours will be granted beginning with the presentation of this note.

"If this proposal should be rejected one German Artillery Corps and six heavy A. A. Battalions are ready to annihilate the U.S.A. Troops in and near Bastogne. The order for firing will be given immediately after this two hour's term.

"All the serious civilian losses caused by this Artillery fire would not correspond with the well known American humanity.

The German Commander"

The German Commander received the following reply:

22 December 1944

"To the German Commander: N U T S !

The American Commander"

Allied Troops are counterattacking in force. We continue to hold Bastogne. By holding Bastogne we assure the success of the Allied Armies. We know that our Division Commander, General Taylor, will say: "Well Done!"

We are giving our country and our loved ones at home a worthy Christmas present and being privileged to take part in this gallant feat of arms are truly making ourselves a Merry Christmas.

(signed)
McAULIFFE,
Commanding.

─────────────── **Instrument of German Surrender** ───────────────

World War II began in the early morning hours of September 1, 1939, and for Germany, who started it, it ended in the early morning hours of May 7, 1945. At 0241 hours that day in Rheims, France, the unconditional surrender of "all forces on land, sea, and air" under German authority was signed. The text of that document is reprinted below minus the signatures.

Only this text in English is authoritative

ACT OF MILITARY SURRENDER

1. We the undersigned, acting by authority of the German High Command, hereby surrender unconditionally to the Supreme Commander, Allied Expeditionary Force and simultaneously to the Soviet High Command all forces on land, sea, and in the air who are at this date under German control.

2. The German High Command will at once issue orders to all German military, naval and air authorities and to all forces under German control to cease active operations at 2301 hours Central European time on 8 May and to remain in the positions occupied at that time. No ship, vessel, or aircraft is to be scuttled, or any damage done to their hull, machinery or equipment.

3. The German High Command will at once issue to the appropriate commanders, and ensure the carrying out of any further orders issued by the Supreme Commander, Allied Expeditionary Force and by the Soviet High Command.

4. This act of military surrender is without prejudice to, and will be superseded by any general instrument of surrender imposed by, or on behalf of the United Nations and applicable to GERMANY and the German armed forces as a whole.

5. In the event of the German High Command or any of the forces under their control failing to act in accordance with this Act of Surrender, the Supreme Commander, Allied Expeditionary Force and the Soviet High Command will take such punitive or other action as they deem appropriate.

Signed at Rheims, France, at 0241 hours on the 7th day of May, 1945.

———————Medal of Honor Recipients in World War II———————

The Medal of Honor is the highest award the United States government can give for military valor. Because it is conferred by the President in the name of the Congress, it is commonly called the Congressional Medal of Honor (CMH).

It is bestowed on an individual who distinguishes himself "conspicuously by gallantry and intrepidity at the risk of his life above and beyond the call of duty."

The award was conceived in the 1860s and first presented in 1863.

In their provisions for judging whether an individual is entitled to the Medal of Honor, each of the armed services has set up regulations that permit no margin of doubt or error. The deed of the person must be proven by the incontestable evidence of at least two eyewitnesses; it must be so outstanding that it clearly distinguishes his gallantry beyond the call of duty from lesser forms of bravery; it must involve the risk of life; and it must be the type of deed which, if it had not been done, would not subject the individual to any justified criticism.

A history of the Medal of Honor with a list of all recipients from 1863 to 1978 is available from the Superintendent of Documents, U.S. Government Printing Office, Washington, D.C. 20402, for a fee. The list that follows includes all World War II recipients up through October 1983.

Name, Rank, Organization	For Action In or At	Date of Action
Adams, Lucian, Army, Staff Sgt.	St. Die, France	28 Oct. 1944
*Agerholm, Harold C., U.S.M.C., Pfc.	Saipan, Marianas	7 July 1944
Anderson, Beaufort T., Army, Tech. Sgt.	Okinawa	13 Apr. 1945
*Anderson, Richard B., U.S.M.C., Pfc.	Marshall Islands	1 Feb. 1944
*Antolak, Sylvester, Army, Sgt.	Italy	24 May 1944
Antrim, Richard N., Navy, Cmdr.	East Indies	Apr. 1942
Atkins, Thomas E., Army, Pfc.	Philippines	10 Mar. 1945
*Bailey, Kenneth D., U.S.M.C., Maj.	Guadalcanal	12 Sept. 1942
*Baker, Addison E., Army, Lt. Col.	Rumania	1 Aug. 1943

*An asterisk indicates posthumous award.

Name, Rank, Organization	For Action In or At	Date of Action
*Baker, Thomas A., Army, Sgt.	Saipan, Marianas	19 June–7 July 1944
Barfoot, Van T., Army, 2nd Lt.	Carano, Italy	23 May 1944
Barrett, Carlton W., Army, Pvt.	France	6 June 1944
Basilone, John, U.S.M.C., Sgt.	Guadalcanal	24–25 Oct. 1942
*Bauer, Harold W., U.S.M.C., Lt. Col.	South Pacific	10 May–14 Nov. 1942
*Bausell, Lewis K., U.S.M.C., Cpl.	Peleliu Island	15 Sept. 1944
*Beaudoin, Raymond O., Army, 1st Lt.	Germany	6 Apr. 1945
Bell, Bernard P., Army, Tech. Sgt.	France	18 Dec. 1944
Bender, Stanley, Army, Staff Sgt.	France	17 Aug. 1944
*Benjamin, George, Jr., Army, Pfc.	Philippines	21 Dec. 1944
Bennett, Edward A., Army, Cpl.	Germany	1 Feb. 1945
*Bennion, Mervyn S., Navy, Capt.	Pearl Harbor	7 Dec. 1941
*Berry, Charles J., U.S.M.C., Cpl.	Iwo Jima	3 Mar. 1945
Bertoldo, Vito R., Army, Mstr. Sgt.	France	9–10 Jan. 1945
Beyer, Arthur O., Army, Cpl.	Belgium	15 Jan. 1945
*Bianchi, Willibald C., Army, 1st Lt.	Philippines	3 Feb. 1942
Biddle, Melvin E., Army, Pfc.	Belgium	23–24 Dec. 1944
*Bigelow, Elmer C., Navy, Seaman 1/C	Philippines	14 Feb. 1945
Bjorklund, Arnold L., Army, 1st Lt.	Italy	13 Sept. 1943
Bloch, Orville E., Army, 1st Lt.	Italy	22 Sept. 1944
Bolden, Paul L., Army, Staff Sgt.	Belgium	23 Dec. 1944
Bolton, Cecil H., Army, 1st Lt.	Holland	2 Nov. 1944
Bong, Richard I., Army Air Corps, Maj.	Borneo/Leyte	10 Oct.–15 Nov. 1944
*Bonnyman, Alexander, Jr., U.S.M.C., 1st Lt.	Gilbert Islands	20–22 Nov. 1943
*Booker, Robert D., Army, Pvt.	Tunisia	9 Apr. 1943
*Bordelon, William J., U.S.M.C., Sgt.	Gilbert Islands	20 Nov. 1943
*Boyce, George W. G., Jr., Army, 2nd Lt.	New Guinea	23 July 1944
Boyington, Gregory, U.S.M.C., Maj.	Solomon Islands	12 Sept.–3 Jan. 1944
Briles, Herschel F., Army, Staff Sgt.	Germany	20 Nov. 1944
Britt, Maurice L., Army, Capt.	Italy	10 Nov. 1943
*Brostrom, Leonard C., Army, Pfc.	Philippines	28 Oct. 1944
Brown, Bobbie E., Army, Capt.	Germany	8 Oct. 1944
Bulkeley, John D., Navy, Lt. Cmdr.	Philippines	7 Dec./10 Apr. 1942
Burke, Frank, Army, 1st Lt.	Germany	17 Apr. 1945

Q. Who was the first *enlisted* man in the U.S. armed forces to win the Medal of Honor?

A. USMC Sergeant John Basilone for action on Guadalcanal in 1942. He was killed in 1945 on Iwo Jima.

Q. Name the only father and son to both win the Medal of Honor.
A. General Douglas MacArthur in World War II and his father in the
War Between the States.

Name, Rank, Organization	For Action In or At	Date of Action
*Burr, Elmer J., Army, 1st Sgt.	New Guinea	24 Dec. 1942
Burr, Herbert H., Army, Staff Sgt.	Germany	19 Mar. 1945
Burt, James M., Army, Capt.	Germany	13 Oct. 1944
Bush, Richard E., U.S.M.C., Cpl.	Okinawa	16 Apr. 1945
Bush, Robert E., Navy, Med. Corpsman	Okinawa	2 May 1945
*Butts, John E., Army, 2nd Lt.	France	14, 16, 23 June 1944
*Caddy, William R., U.S.M.C., Pfc.	Iwo Jima	3 Mar. 1945
*Callaghan, Daniel J., Navy, Rear Adm.	Savo Island	12–13 Nov. 1942
Calugas, Jose, Army, Sgt.	Philippines	16 Jan. 1942
*Cannon, George H., U.S.M.C., 1st Lt.	Midway	7 Dec. 1941
*Carey, Alvin P., Army, Staff Sgt.	France	23 Aug. 1944
*Carey, Charles F., Jr., Army, Tech. Sgt.	France	8–9 Jan. 1945
Carr, Chris, Army, Sgt.	Italy	1–2 Oct. 1944
(legally changed from Christos H. Karaberis, name under which medal was awarded)		
*Carswell, H. S., Jr., Army Air Corps, Maj.	S. China Sea	26 Oct. 1944
Casamento, Anthony, U.S.M.C., Cpl.	Guadalcanal	1 Nov. 1942
*Castle, Frederick W.,		
Army Air Corps., Brig. Gen./Asst. Cmdr.	Germany	24 Dec. 1944
Chambers, Justice M., U.S.M.C., Col.	Iwo Jima	19–22 Feb. 1945
*Cheli, Ralph, Army Air Corps, Maj.	New Guinea	18 Aug. 1943
Childers, Ernest, Army, 2nd Lt.	Italy	22 Sept. 1943
Choate, Clyde L., Army, Staff Sgt.	France	25 Oct. 1944
*Christensen, Dale E., Army, 2nd Lt.	New Guinea	16–19 July 1944
*Christian, Herbert F., Army, Pvt.	Italy	2–3 June 1944
*Cicchetti, Joseph J., Army, Pfc.	Philippines	9 Feb. 1945
Clark, Francis J., Army, Tech. Sgt.	Luxembourg	12 Sept. 1944
Colalillo, Mike, Army, Pfc.	Germany	7 Apr. 1945
*Cole, Darrell S., U.S.M.C., Sgt.	Iwo Jima	19 Feb. 1945
*Cole, Robert G., Army (Airborne), Lt. Col.	France	11 June 1944
Connor, James P., Army, Sgt.	France	15 Aug. 1944
Cooley, Raymond H., Army, Staff Sgt.	Philippines	24 Feb. 1945
Coolidge, Charles H., Army, Tech. Sgt.	France	24–27 Oct. 1944
*Courtney, Henry A., Jr., U.S.M.C., Maj.	Ryukyu Islands	14–15 May 1945
*Cowan, Richard E., Army, Pfc.	Belgium	17 Dec. 1944
Craft, Clarence B.. Army, Pfc.	Okinawa	31 May 1945

Name, Rank, Organization	For Action In or At	Date of Action
*Craig, Robert, Army, 2nd Lt.	Sicily	11 July 1943
*Crain, Morris E., Army, Tech. Sgt.	France	13 Mar. 1945
*Craw, Demas T., Army Air Corps, Col.	French Morocco	8 Nov. 1942
Crawford, William J., Army, Pvt.	Italy	13 Sept. 1943
Crews, John R., Army, Staff Sgt.	Germany	8 Apr. 1945
*Cromwell, John P., Navy, Capt.	Pacific	19 Nov. 1943
Currey, Francis S., Army, Sgt.	Belgium	21 Dec. 1944
Dahlgren, Edward C., Army, 2nd Lt.	France	11 Feb. 1945
Dalessondro, Peter J., Army, Tech. Sgt.	Germany	22 Dec. 1944
Daly, Michael J., Army, Capt.	Nuremberg, Germany	18 Apr. 1945
*Damato, Anthony P., U.S.M.C., Cpl.	Marshall Islands	19–20 Feb. 1944
*David, Albert L., Navy, Lt. (jg)	French West Africa	4 June 1944
Davis, Charles W., Army, Maj.	Guadalcanal	12 Jan. 1943
*Davis, George F., Navy, Cmdr.	Philippines	6 Jan. 1945
*Dealey, Samuel D., Navy, Cmdr.	Enemy waters	Various dates
DeBlanc, Jefferson J., U.S.M.C., Capt.	Solomon Islands	31 Jan. 1943
*DeFranzo, Arthur F., Army, Staff Sgt.	Vaubadon, France	10 June 1944
*DeGlopper, Charles N., Army, Pfc.	France	9 June 1944
*Deleau, Emile, Jr., Army, Sgt.	Oberhoffen, France	1–2 Feb. 1945
Dervishian, Ernest H., Army, 2nd Lt.	Cisterna, Italy	23 May 1944
*Diamond, James H., Army, Pfc.	Philippines	8–14 May 1945
*Dietz, Robert H., Army, Staff Sgt.	Kirchain, Germany	29 Mar. 1945
Doolittle, James H., Army, Brig. Gen.	Japan	9 June 1942
Doss, Desmond T., Army, Pfc.	Okinawa	29 Apr.–21 May 1945
Drowley, Jesse R., Army, Staff Sgt.	Solomon Islands	30 Jan. 1944
Dunham, Russell E., Army, Tech. Sgt.	France	8 Jan. 1945
Dunlop, Robert H., U.S.M.C., Capt.	Iwo Jima	20–21 Feb. 1945
*Dutko, John W., Army, Pfc.	Italy	23 May 1944
*Dyess, Aquilla J., U.S.M.C., Lt. Col.	Marshall Islands	1–2 Feb. 1944
Edson, Merritt A., U.S.M.C., Col.	Solomon Islands	13–14 Sept. 1942

FACT American propaganda frequently called the Japanese kamikaze, or suicide plane, pilots fanatics, while at the same time U.S. military personnel who performed similarly were regarded as heroes. Captain Richard E. Fleming, a U.S. Marine Corps pilot, posthumously received the Medal of Honor for diving his flaming bomber onto the deck of the Japanese cruiser *Mikuma* during the Battle of Midway. Some reference works report his act as the first such personal sacrifice in the Pacific war.

Q. Who was the most decorated U.S. paratrooper in the war?
A. Sergeant Leonard A. Funk, 508th Parachute Infantry Regiment, 82nd Airborne Division, who received the Medal of Honor, the Distinguished Service Cross and several other decorations. (See Volume 1, page 105).

Name, Rank, Organization	For Action In or At	Date of Action
Ehlers, Walter D., Army, Staff Sgt.	France	9–10 June 1944
*Elrod, Henry T., U.S.M.C., Capt.	Wake Island	8–23 Dec. 1941
*Endl, Gerald L., Army, Staff Sgt.	New Guinea	11 July 1944
*Epperson, Harold G., U.S.M.C., Pfc.	Saipan, Marianas	25 June 1944
Erwin, Henry E., Army Air Corps, Staff Sgt.	Koriyama, Japan	12 Apr. 1945
*Eubanks, Ray E., Army, Sgt.	Dutch New Guinea	23 July 1944
*Evans, Ernest E., Navy, Cmdr.	Samar	25 Oct. 1944
Everhart, Forrest E., Army, Tech. Sgt.	Kerling, France	12 Nov. 1944
*Fardy, John P., U.S.M.C., Cpl.	Okinawa	7 May 1945
*Femoyer, Robert E., Army Air Corps, 2nd Lt.	Merseburg, Germany	2 Nov. 1944
Fields, James H., Army, 1st Lt.	France	27 Sept. 1944
Finn, John W., Navy, Lt.	Kaneche Bay, Hawaii	7 Dec. 1941
Fisher, Almond E., Army, 2nd Lt.	France	12–13 Sept. 1944
*Flaherty, Francis C., Navy, Ens.	Pearl Harbor	7 Dec. 1941
*Fleming, Richard E., U.S.M.C., Capt.	Midway	4–5 June 1942
Fluckey, Eugene B., Navy, Cmdr.	Coast of China	19 Dec.–15 Feb. 1945
Foss, Joseph J., U.S.M.C., Capt.	Guadalcanal	9 Oct.–19 Nov. 1942 15–23 Jan. 1943
*Foster, William A., Marine Res., Pfc.	Okinawa	2 May 1945
*Fournier, William G., Army, Sgt.	Guadalcanal	10 Jan. 1943
*Fowler, Thomas W., Army, 2nd Lt.	Carano, Italy	23 May 1944
*Fryar, Elmer E., Army, Pvt.	Philippines	8 Dec. 1944
Funk, Leonard A., Jr., Army, 1st Sgt.	Belgium	29 Jan. 1945
Fuqua, Samuel G., Navy, Capt.	Pearl Harbor	7 Dec. 1941
Galer, Robert E., U.S.M.C., Maj.	Solomon Islands	Various dates
*Galt, William W., Army, Capt.	Italy	29 May 1944
*Gammon, Archer T., Army, Staff Sgt.	Belgium	11 Jan. 1945
Garcia, Marcario, Army, Staff Sgt.	Germany	27 Nov. 1944
Garman, Harold A., Army, Pvt.	France	25 Aug. 1944
Gary, Donald A., Navy, Lt. (jg)	Kobe, Japan	19 Mar. 1945
Gerstung, Robert E., Army, Tech. Sgt.	Berg, Germany	19 Dec. 1944
*Gibson, Eric G., Army, T/5	Italy	28 Jan. 1944
*Gilmore, Howard W., Navy, Cmdr.	Southwest Pacific	10 Jan.–7 Feb. 1943

FACT One of the widest-held pieces of misinformation concerning the war is that Captain Colin P. Kelly, Jr., received the Medal of Honor for his actions following the sinking of the Japanese battleship *Haruna*. Kelly did not sink the battleship nor did he receive the CMH. The *Haruna* was sunk by aircraft off Kure, Japan, on July 28, 1945. Kelly was awarded a posthumous Distinguished Service Cross for remaining in his aircraft while his B-17 crew bailed out on December 10, 1942.

Name, Rank, Organization	For Action In or At	Date of Action
*Gonsalves, Harold, U.S.M.C., Pfc.	Okinawa	15 Apr. 1945
*Gonzales, David M., Army, Pfc.	Philippines	25 Apr. 1945
Gordon, Nathan G., Navy, Lt.	Bismarck Sea	15 Feb. 1944
*Gott, Donald J., Army Air Corps, 1st Lt.	Germany	9 Nov. 1944
*Grabiarz, William J., Army, Pfc.	Philippines	23 Feb. 1945
*Gray, Ross F., U.S.M.C., Sgt.	Iwo Jima	21 Feb. 1945
Gregg, Stephen R., Army, 2nd Lt.	France	27 Aug. 1944
*Gruennert, Kenneth E., Army, Sgt.	Buna, New Guinea	24 Dec. 1942
*Gurke, Henry, U.S.M.C., Pfc.	Solomon Islands	9 Nov. 1943
Hall, George J., Army, Staff Sgt.	Anzio, Italy	23 May 1944
*Hall, Lewis, Army, T/5	Guadalcanal	10 Jan. 1943
Hall, William E., Navy, Lt. (jg)	Coral Sea	7–8 May 1942
*Hallman, Sherwood H., Army, Staff Sgt.	France	13 Sept. 1944
*Halyburton, W. D., Jr., Navy, Pharm. Mate	Okinawa	10 May 1945
Hamilton, Pierpont M., Army Air Corps, Maj.	French Morocco	8 Nov. 1942
*Hammerberg, Owen, Navy, Boatswain's Mate	Pearl Harbor	17 Feb. 1945
*Hansen, Dale M., U.S.M.C., Pvt.	Okinawa	7 May 1945
*Hanson, Robert M., U.S.M.C., 1st Lt.	Bougainville	1 Nov. 1943
*Harmon, Roy W., Army, Sgt.	Casaglia	12 July 1944
*Harr, Harry R., Army, Cpl.	Philippines	5 June 1945
Harrell, William G., U.S.M.C., Sgt	Iwo Jima	3 Mar. 1945
*Harris, James L., Army, 2nd Lt.	Vagney, France	7 Oct. 1944
*Hastings, Joe R., Army, Pfc.	Germany	14 May 1945
*Hauge, Louis J., Jr., U.S.M.C., Cpl.	Ryukyus	14 May 1945
Hawk, John D., Army, Sgt.	France	20 Aug. 1944
*Hawkins, William D., U.S.M.C., 1st Lt.	Gilbert Islands	20–21 Nov. 1943
Hawks, Lloyd C., Army, Pfc.	Italy	30 Jan. 1944
*Hedrick, Clinton M., Army, Tech. Sgt.	Germany	27–28 Mar. 1945
Hendrix, James R., Army, Pvt.	Belgium	26 Dec. 1944
*Henry, Robert T., Army, Pvt.	Germany	3 Dec. 1944

Name, Rank, Organization	For Action In or At	Date of Action
Herrera, Silvestre S., Army, Pfc.	France	15 Mar. 1945
Herring, Rufus G., Navy, Lt.	Iwo Jima	17 Feb. 1945
*Hill, Edwin J., Navy, Chief Boatswain	Pearl Harbor	7 Dec. 1941
Horner, Freeman V., Army Staff Sgt.	Germany	16 Nov. 1944
Howard, James H., Army Air Corps, Lt. Col.	Germany	11 Jan. 1944
Huff, Paul B., Army, Cpl.	Italy	8 Feb. 1944
*Hughes, Lloyd H., Army Air Corps, 2nd Lt.	Rumania	1 Aug. 1943
*Hutchins, J.D., Navy, Seaman 1/C	New Guinea	4 Sept. 1943
*Jachman, Isadore S., Army, Staff Sgt.	Belgium	4 Jan. 1945
Jackson, Arthur J., U.S.M.C., Pfc.	Peleliu	18 Sept. 1944
Jacobson, Douglas T., U.S.M.C., Pfc.	Iwo Jima	26 Feb. 1945
*Jerstad, John L., Army Air Corps, Maj.	Rumania	1 Aug. 1943
*Johnson, Elden H., Army, Pvt.	Italy	3 June 1944
Johnson, Leon W., Army Air Corps, Col.	Rumania	1 Aug. 1943
*Johnson, Leroy, Army, Sgt.	Philippines	15 Dec. 1944
Johnson, Oscar G., Army, Sgt.	Italy	16–18 Sept. 1944
Johnston, William J., Army, Pfc.	Italy	17–19 Feb. 1944
*Jones, Herbert C., Navy, Ens.	Pearl Harbor	7 Dec. 1941
*Julian, Joseph R., U.S.M.C., Sgt.	Iwo Jima	9 Mar. 1945
*Kandle, Victor L., Army, 1st Lt.	France	9 Oct. 1944
Kane, John R., Army Air Corps, Col.	Rumania	1 Aug. 1943
Kearby, Neel E., Army Air Corps, Col.	New Guinea	11 Oct. 1943
*Keathley, George D., Army, Staff Sgt.	Italy	14 Sept. 1944
*Kefurt, Gus, Army, Staff Sgt.	France	23–24 Dec. 1944
*Kelley, Jonah E., Army, Staff Sgt.	Germany	30–31 Jan. 1945
*Kelley, Ova A., Army, Pvt.	Philippines	8 Dec. 1944
Kelly, Charles E., Army, Cpl.	Italy	13 Sept. 1943
*Kelly, John D., Army, Tech. Sgt.	France	25 June 1944
Kelly, Thomas J., Army, Cpl.	Germany	5 Apr. 1945
*Keppler, R.J., Navy, Boatswain's Mate	Solomon Islands	12–13 Nov. 1942
Kerstetter, Dexter J., Army, Pfc.	Philippines	13 Apr. 1945
*Kessler, Patrick L., Army, Pfc.	Italy	23 May 1944
*Kidd, Isaac C., Navy, Rear Adm.	Pearl Harbor	7 Dec. 1941
*Kimbro, Truman, Army, T/4	Belgium	19 Dec. 1944

Q. Name the only Pulitzer Prize winner who also won the Medal of Honor.

A. American aviation legend Charles A. Lindbergh. (Volume 1, pages 72 and 80)

Name, Rank, Organization	For Action In or At	Date of Action
*Kiner, Harold G., Army, Pvt.	Germany	2 Oct. 1944
*Kingsley, David R., Army Air Corps, 2nd Lt.	Rumania	23 June 1944
*Kinser, Elbert L. U.S.M.C., Sgt.	Ryukyus	4 May 1945
Kisters, Gerry H., Army, 2nd Lt.	Sicily	31 July 1943
Knappenberger, Alton W., Army, Pfc.	Italy	1 Feb. 1944
*Knight, Jack L., Army, 1st Lt.	Loi–Kang, Burma	2 Feb. 1945
*Knight, R. L., Army Air Corps, 1st Lt.	Italy	24–25 Apr. 1945
*Kraus, Richard E., U.S.M.C., Pfc.	Palau Islands	5 Oct. 1944
*Krotiak, Anthony L., Army, Pfc.	Philippines	8 May 1945
*LaBelle, James D., U.S.M.C., Pfc.	Iwo Jima	8 Mar. 1945
Lawley, W. R., Jr., Army Air Corps, 1st Lt.	Over Europe	20 Feb. 1944
Laws, Robert E., Army, Staff Sgt.	Philippines	12 Jan. 1945
Lee, Daniel W., Army, 1st Lt.	France	2 Sept. 1944
Leims, John H., U.S.M.C., 2nd Lt.	Iwo Jima	7 Mar. 1945
*Leonard, Turney W., Army, 1st Lt.	Germany	4–6 Nov. 1944
*Lester, Fred F., Navy, Hosp. 1/C	Ryukyus	8 June 1945
*Lindsey, Darrel R., Army Air Corps, Capt.	France	9 Aug. 1944
Linsey, Jake W., Army, Tech. Sgt.	Germany	16 Nov. 1944
*Lindstrom, Floyd K., Army, Pfc.	Italy	11 Nov. 1943
*Lloyd, Edgar H., Army, 1st Lt.	France	14 Sept. 1944
*Lobaugh, Donald R., Army, Pvt.	New Guinea	22 July 1944
Logan, James M., Army, Sgt.	Italy	9 Sept. 1943
Lopez, Jose M., Army, Sgt.	Belgium	17 Dec. 1944
Lucas, Jacklyn H., U.S.M.C., Pfc.	Iwo Jima	20 Feb. 1945
*Lummus, Jack, U.S.M.C., 1st Lt.	Iwo Jima	8 Mar. 1945
Mabry, George L., Jr., Army, Lt. Col.	Germany	20 Nov. 1944
MacArthur, Douglas, Army, Gen.	Philippines	
MacGillivary, Charles A., Army, Sgt.	France	1 Jan. 1945
*Magrath, John D., Army, Pfc.	Italy	14 Apr. 1945
*Mann, Joe E., Army, Pfc.	Holland	18 Sept. 1944
*Martin, Harry L., U.S.M.C., 1st Lt.	Iwo Jima	26 Mar. 1945
*Martinez, Joe P., Army, Pvt.	Aleutians	26 May 1943
*Mason, Leonard F., U.S.M.C., Pfc.	Guam	22 July 1944

Q. Identify the U.S. Marine who received the last Medal of Honor authorized by Congress *during* the war.

A. Private First Class Robert M. McTureous, Jr., for action on Okinawa. (Congress authorized other medals *after* the actual fighting stopped.)

Name, Rank, Organization	For Action In or At	Date of Action
*Mathies, Archibald, Army Air Corps, Sgt.	Over Europe	20 Feb. 1944
*Mathis, Jack W., Army Air Corps, 1st Lt.	Germany	18 Mar. 1943
Maxwell, Robert D., Army, T/5	France	7 Sept. 1944
*May, Martin O., Army, Pfc.	Ryukyus	19–21 Apr. 1945
Mayfield, Melvin, Army, Cpl.	Philippines	29 July 1945
McCall, Thomas E., Army, Staff Sgt.	Italy	22 Jan. 1944
McCampbell, David, Navy, Cmdr.	Philippine Sea	19 June 1944
McCandless, Bruce, Navy, Cmdr.	Savo Island	12–13 Nov. 1942
*McCard, Robert H., U.S.M.C., Gun. Sgt.	Saipan, Marianas	16 June 1944
McCarter, Lloyd G., Army, Pvt.	Philippines	16–19 Feb. 1945
McCarthy, Joseph J., U.S.M.C., Capt.	Iwo Jima	21 Feb. 1945
McCool, Richard M., Jr., Navy, Lt.	Off Okinawa	10–11 June 1945
McGaha, Charles L., Army, Mstr. Sgt.	Philippines	7 Feb. 1945
McGarity, Vernon, Army, Tech. Sgt.	Belgium	16 Dec. 1944
*McGee, William D., Army, Pvt.	Mülheim, Germany	18 Mar. 1945
*McGill, Troy A., Army, Sgt.	Los Negros Islands	4 Mar. 1944
*McGraw, Francis X., Army, Pfc.	Germany	19 Nov. 1944
*McGuire, T. B., Jr., Army Air Corps, Maj.	Philippines	25–26 Dec. 1944
McKinney, John R., Army, Sgt.	Philippines	11 May 1945
*McTureous, Robert M., Jr., U.S.M.C., Pvt.	Okinawa	7 June 1945
*McVeigh, John J., Army, Sgt.	France	29 Aug. 1944
*McWhorter, William A., Army, Pfc.	Philippines	5 Dec. 1944
Meagher, John, Army, Tech. Sgt.	Okinawa	19 June 1945
Merli, Gino J., Army, Pfc.	Belgium	4–5 Sept. 1944
*Merrell, Joseph F., Army, Pvt.	Germany	18 Apr. 1945
*Messerschmidt, Harold O., Army, Sgt.	France	17 Sept. 1944
*Metzger, W. E., Jr., Army Air Corps, 2nd Lt.	Germany	9 Nov. 1944
Michael, Edward S., Army Air Corps, 1st Lt.	Over Germany	11 Apr. 1944
*Michael, Harry J., Army, 2nd Lt.	Germany	14 Mar. 1945
*Miller, Andrew, Army, Staff Sgt.	France/Germany	16–29 Nov. 1944
Mills, James H., Army, Pvt.	Italy	24 May 1944
*Minick, John W., Army, Staff Sgt.	Germany	21 Nov. 1944
*Minue, Nicholas, Army, Pvt.	Tunisia	28 Apr. 1943
*Monteith, Jimmie W., Jr., Army, 1st Lt.	France	6 June 1944
Montgomery, Jack C., Army, 1st Lt.	Italy	22 Feb. 1944
*Moon, Harold H., Jr., Army, Pvt.	Philippines	21 Oct. 1944
Morgan, John C., Army Air Corps, 2nd Lt.	Over Europe	28 July 1943
*Moskala, Edward J., Army, Pfc.	Okinawa	9 Apr. 1945
*Mower, Charles E., Army, Sgt.	Philippines	3 Nov. 1944

Name, Rank, Organization	For Action In or At	Date of Action
*Muller, Joseph E., Army, Sgt.	Okinawa	15–16 May 1945
*Munemori, Sadao S., Army, Pfc.	Italy	5 Apr. 1945
*Munro, D. A., Coast Guard, Signalman 1/C	Guadalcanal	27 Sept. 1942
Murphy, Audie L., Army, 2nd Lt.	France	26 Jan. 1945
*Murphy, Frederick C., Army, Pfc.	Germany	18 Mar. 1945
Murray, Charles P., Jr., Army, 1st Lt.	France	16 Dec. 1944
*Nelson, William L., Army, Sgt.	Djebel Dardys	24 Apr. 1943
Neppel, Ralph G., Army, Sgt.	Birgel, Germany	14 Dec. 1944
Nett, Robert P., Army, Capt.	Philippines	14 Dec. 1944
*New, John D., U.S.M.C., Pfc.	Peleliu	25 Sept. 1944
Newman, Beryl R., Army, 1st Lt.	Cisterna, Italy	26 May 1944
*Nininger, A. R., Jr., Army, 2nd Lt.	Philippines	12 Jan. 1942
*O'Brien, William J., Army, Lt. Col.	Marianas Islands	20 June–7 July 1944
O'Callahan, J. T., Navy, Cmdr.	Japan	19 Mar. 1945
Ogden, Carlos C., Army, 1st Lt.	France	25 June 1944
O'Hare, Edward H., Navy, Lt.	Pacific	20 Feb. 1942
O'Kane, Richard H., Navy, Cmdr.	Philippines	23–24 Oct. 1944
*Olson, Arlo L., Army, Capt.	Italy	13 Oct. 1943
*Olson, Truman O., Army, Sgt.	Italy	30–31 Jan. 1944
Oresko, Nicholas, Army Mstr. Sgt.	Germany	23 Jan. 1945
*Owens, Robert A., U.S.M.C., Sgt.	Solomon Islands	1 Nov. 1943
*Ozbourn, Joseph W., U.S.M.C., Pvt.	Marianas Islands	30 July 1944
Paige, Mitchell, U.S.M.C., Sgt.	Solomon Isls.	26 Oct. 1942
*Parle, John J., Navy, Ens.	Italy	9–10 July 1943
*Parrish, Laverne, Army, T/4	Philippines	18–24 Jan. 1945
*Pease, Harl, Jr., Army Air Corps, Capt.	New Britain	6–7 Aug. 1942
*Peden, Forrest E., Army, T/5	France	3 Feb. 1945
*Pendleton, Jack J., Army, Staff Sgt.	Germany	12 Oct. 1944
*Peregory, Frank D., Army, Tech. Sgt.	France	8 June 1944
*Perez, Manuel, Jr., Army, Pfc.	Philippines	13 Feb. 1945
*Peters, George J., Army, Pvt.	Germany	24 Mar. 1945
*Peterson, George, Army, Staff Sgt.	Germany	30 Mar. 1945
*Peterson, Oscar V., Navy, Chief Watertender	Pacific	7 May 1942

Q. Name the first U.S. serviceman to be awarded a Medal of Honor
in the war.

A. Lieutenant Alexander R. Nininger, Jr., killed on Luzon in the Philippines early in the war, received the citation posthumously, for action on January 12, 1942, near Abucay, Bataan.

Q. Identify the only chaplain in the war to receive a Medal of Honor.

A. U.S. Navy Chaplain Joseph O'Callahan. He earned the distinction for heroism aboard the aircraft carrier USS *Franklin* (CV-13) when the "ship that wouldn't die" went through its ordeal in March 1945.

Name, Rank, Organization	For Action In or At	Date of Action
*Petrarca, Frank J., Army, Pfc.	Solomon Islands	27 July 1943
Pharris, Jackson C., Navy, Lt.	Pearl Harbor	7 Dec. 1941
*Phelps, Wesley, U.S.M.C., Pvt.	Peleliu	4 Oct. 1944
*Phillips, George, U.S.M.C., Pvt.	Iwo Jima	14 Mar. 1945
Pierce, F. J., Navy, Pharm. Mate 1/C	Iwo Jima	15–16 Mar. 1945
*Pinder, John J., Jr., Army T/5	France	6 June 1944
Pope, Everett P., U.S.M.C., Capt.	Peleliu	19–20 Sept. 1944
*Power, John V., U.S.M.C., 1st Lt.	Namur Island	1 Feb. 1944
*Powers, John J., Navy, Lt.	Coral Sea	4–8 May 1942
Powers, Leo J., Army, Pfc.	Italy	3 Feb. 1944
Preston, Arthur M., Navy, Lt.	Halmahera Islands	16 Sept. 1944
*Prussman, Earnest W., Army, Pfc.	France	8 Sept. 1944
*Pucket, D. D., Army Air Corps, 1st Lt.	Rumania	9 July 1944
Ramage, Lawson P., Navy, Cmdr.	Pacific	31 July 1944
*Ray, Bernard J., Army, 1st Lt.	Germany	17 Nov. 1944
*Reese, James W., Army, Pvt.	Italy	5 Aug. 1943
*Reese, John N., Jr., Army, Pfc.	Philippines	9 Feb. 1945
*Reeves, Thomas J., Navy, Radio Elect.	Pearl Harbor	7 Dec. 1941
*Ricketts, Milton E., Navy, Lt.	Coral Sea	8 May 1942
*Riordan, Paul F., Army, 2nd Lt.	Italy	3–8 Feb. 1944
*Roan, Charles H., U.S.M.C., Pfc.	Palau Islands	18 Sept. 1944
*Robinson, J. E., Jr., Army, 1st Lt.	Germany	6 Apr. 1945
Rodriguez, Cleto, Army, Tech. Sgt.	Philippines	9 Feb. 1945
*Roeder, Robert E., Army, Capt.	Italy	27–28 Sept. 1944
*Rooks, Albert H., Navy, Capt.	Pacific	4–27 Feb. 1942
*Roosevelt, Theodore, Jr., Army, Brig. Gen.	France	6 June 1944
Ross, Donald Kirby, Navy, Mach.	Pearl Harbor	7 Dec. 1941
Ross, Wilburn K., Army, Pvt.	France	30 Oct. 1944
Rouh, Carlton R., U.S.M.C., 1st Lt.	Peleliu	15 Sept. 1944
Rudolph, Donald E., Army, 2nd Lt.	Philippines	5 Feb. 1945
*Ruhl, Donald J., U.S.M.C., Pfc.	Iwo Jima	19–21 Feb. 1945
Ruiz, Alejandro R. R., Army, Pfc.	Okinawa	28 Apr. 1945
*Sadowski, Joseph J., Army, Sgt.	France	14 Sept. 1944
*Sarnoski, J. R., Army Air Corps, 2nd Lt.	Solomon Islands	16 June 1943

Name, Rank, Organization	For Action In or At	Date of Action
*Sayers, Foster J., Army, Pfc.	France	12 Nov. 1944
Schaefer, Joseph E., Army, Staff Sgt.	Germany	
Schauer, Henry, Army, Pfc.	Italy	23–24 May 1944
Schonland, Herbert E., Navy, Cmdr.	Savo Island	12–13 Nov. 1943
*Schwab, Albert E., U.S.M.C., Pfc.	Okinawa	7 May 1945
*Scott, Norman, Navy, Rear Adm.	Savo Island	11–12 Oct. & 12–13 Nov. 1942
*Scott, Robert R., Navy, Machinist's Mate	Pearl Harbor	7 Dec. 1941
Scott, Robert S., Army, Capt.	Solomon Islands	29 July 1943
Shea, Charles W., Army, 2nd Lt.	Italy	12 May 1944
*Sheridan, Carl V., Army, Pfc.	Germany	26 Nov. 1944
*Shockley, William R., Army, Pfc.	Philippines	31 Mar. 1945
Shomo, William A., Army Air Corps, Maj.	Philippines	11 Jan. 1945
*Shoup, Curtis F., Army, Staff Sgt.	Belgium	7 Jan. 1945
Shoup, David M., U.S.M.C., Col.	Gilbert Islands	20–22 Nov. 1943
Sigler, Franklin E., U.S.M.C., Pvt.	Iwo Jima	14 Mar. 1945
Silk, Edward A., Army, 1st Lt.	France	23 Nov. 1944
Sjogren, John C., Army, Staff Sgt.	Philippines	23 May 1945
Skaggs, Luther, Jr., U.S.M.C., Pfc.	Marianas Islands	21–22 July 1944
Slaton, James D., Army, Cpl.	Italy	23 Sept. 1943
*Smith, Furman L., Army, Pvt.	Italy	31 May 1944
Smith, John L., U.S.M.C., Maj.	Solomon Islands	Aug.–Sept. 1942
Smith, Maynard H., Army Air Corps, Sgt.	Over Europe	1 May 1943
Soderman, William A., Army, Pfc.	Belgium	17 Dec. 1944
Sorenson, Richard K., U.S.M.C., Pvt.	Marshall Islands	1–2 Feb. 1944
*Specker, Joe C., Army, Sgt.	Italy	7 Jan. 1944
Spurrier, Junior J., Army, Staff Sgt.	France	13 Nov. 1944
*Squires, John C., Army, Sgt.	Italy	23–24 Apr. 1944

Q. Identify the U.S. pilot who is credited with shooting down seven enemy aircraft on his first mission.

A. Captain (later major) William A. Shomo received the Medal of Honor for the feat on January 11, 1945, over Luzon in the Philippines. Shomo was lead pilot in a flight of two planes on a photographic mission when they encountered a Japanese twin-engine bomber and a twelve-fighter escort. Shomo maneuvered and attacked several times and shot down seven aircraft including the bomber. The other U.S. plane shot down three, and the remaining three enemy aircraft escaped in a cloudbank. In civilian life Shomo was a mortician.

Name, Rank, Organization	For Action In or At	Date of Action
*Stein, Tony, U.S.M.C., Cpl.	Iwo Jima	19 Feb. 1945
Street, George L. III, Navy, Cmdr.	Quelpart Island	14 Apr. 1945
*Stryker, Stuart S., Army, Pfc.	Germany	24 Mar. 1945
Swett, James E., U.S.M.C., 1st Lt.	Solomon Islands	7 Apr. 1943
*Terry, Seymour W., Army, Capt.	Okinawa	11 May 1945
*Thomas, Herbert J., U.S.M.C., Sgt.	Solomon Islands	7 Nov. 1943
*Thomas, William H., Army, Pfc.	Philippines	22 Apr. 1945
*Thomason, Clyde, U.S.M.C., Sgt.	Makin Island	17–18 Aug. 1942
Thompson, Max, Army, Sgt.	Germany	18 Oct. 1944
*Thorne, Horace M., Army, Cpl.	Belgium	21 Dec. 1944
*Thorson, John F., Army, Pfc.	Philippines	28 Oct. 1944
*Timmerman, Grant F., U.S.M.C., Sgt.	Marianas Islands	8 July 1944
*Tomich, Peter, Navy, Ch. Watertender	Pearl Harbor	7 Dec. 1941
Tominac, John J., Army, 1st Lt.	France	12 Sept. 1944
*Towle, John R., Army, Pvt.	Holland	21 Sept. 1944
Treadwell, Jack L., Army, Capt.	Germany	18 Mar. 1945
*Truemper, W. E. Army Air Corps, 2nd Lt.	Over Europe	20 Feb. 1944
*Turner, Day G., Army, Sgt.	Luxembourg	8 Jan. 1945
Turner, George B., Army, Pfc.	France	3 Jan. 1945
Urban, Matt, Army, Capt.	France	14 June–3 Sept. 1944
*Valdez, Jose F., Army, Pfc.	France	25 Jan. 1945
*Vance, L. R., Jr., Army Air Corps, Lt. Col.	France	5 June 1944
Vandergrift, Alex A., U.S.M.C., Maj. Gen.	Solomon Islands	7 Aug.–9 Dec. 1942
*Van Noy, Junior, Army, Pvt.	New Guinea	17 Oct. 1943
*Van Valkenburgh, Franklin, Navy, Capt.	Pearl Harbor	7 Dec. 1941
*Van Voorhis, Bruce A., Navy, Lt. Cmdr.	Solomon Islands	6 July 1943
*Viale, Robert M., Army, 2nd Lt.	Philippines	5 Feb. 1945
*Villegas, Ysmael R., Army, Staff Sgt.	Philippines	20 Mar. 1945
Vlug, Dirk J., Army, Pfc.	Philippines	15 Dec. 1944
Vosler, F. T., Army Air Corps, Tech. Sgt.	Germany	20 Dec. 1943
Wahlen, George E., Navy, Pharm. Mate	Iwo Jima	3 Mar. 1945
Wainwright, Jonathan M., Army, Gen.	Philippines	12 Mar.–7 May 1942
*Walker, K. N., Army Air Corps, Brig. Gen.	New Britain	5 Jan. 1943
*Wallace, Herman C., Army, Pfc.	Germany	27 Feb. 1945
Walsh, Kenneth A., U.S.M.C., 1st Lt.	Solomon Islands	15 & 30 Aug. 1943
*Walsh, William G., U.S.M.C. Res., Gun/Sgt.	Iwo Jima	27 Feb. 1945
*Ward, James R., Navy, Seaman 1/C	Pearl Harbor	7 Dec. 1941
Ware, Keith L., Army, Lt. Col.	France	26 Dec. 1944
*Warner, Henry F., Army, Cpl.	Belgium	20–21 Dec. 1944

Name, Rank, Organization	For Action In or At	Date of Action
Watson, Wilson D., U.S.M.C., Pvt.	Iwo Jima	26–27 Feb. 1945
*Waugh, Robert T., Army, 1st Lt.	Italy	11–14 May 1944
Waybur, David C., Army, 1st Lt.	Italy	17 July 1943
*Weicht, Ellis R., Army, Sgt.	France	3 Dec. 1944
*Wetzel, Walter C., Army, Pfc.	Germany	3 Apr. 1945
Whiteley, Eli, Army, 1st Lt.	France	27 Dec. 1944
Whittington, Hulon B., Army, Sgt.	France	29 July 1944
Wiedorfer, Paul J., Army, Staff Sgt.	Belgium	25 Dec. 1944
*Wigle, Thomas W., Army, 2nd Lt.	Italy	14 Sept. 1944
Wilbur, William H., Army, Col.	North Africa	8 Nov. 1942
*Wilkin, Edward G., Army, Cpl.	Germany	18 Mar. 1945
*Wilkins, Raymond H., Army Air Corps, Maj.	New Britain	2 Nov. 1943
*Will, Walter J., Army, 1st Lt.	Germany	30 Mar. 1945
Williams, Hershel W., U.S.M.C., Cpl.	Volcano Islands	23 Feb. 1945
*Williams, Jack, Navy, Pharm. Mate 3/C	Volcano Islands	3 March 1945
*Willis, J. H., Navy, Pharm. Mate 1/C	Volcano Islands	28 Feb. 1945
*Wilson, Alfred L., Army, T/5	France	8 Nov. 1944
Wilson, Louis Hugh, Jr., U.S.M.C., Capt.	Guam	25–26 July 1944
*Wilson, Robert L., U.S.M.C., Pfc.	Tinian Island	4 Aug. 1944
Wise, Homer L., Army, Staff Sgt.	Italy	14 June 1944
*Witek, Frank P., U.S.M.C., Pfc.	Marianas Islands	3 Aug. 1944
*Woodford, Howard E., Army, Staff Sgt.	Philippines	6 June 1945
Young, Cassin, Navy, Cmdr.	Pearl Harbor	7 Dec. 1941
*Young, Rodger W., Army, Pvt.	Solomon Islands	31 July 1943
Zeamer, Jay, Jr., Army Air Corps, Maj.	Solomon Islands	16 June 1943
*Zussman, Raymond, Army, 2nd Lt.	France	12 Sept. 1944

Bibliography

Aldeman, Robert H. and Walton, George. *The Devil's Brigade*. Philadelphia: Chilton, 1966.

Ambrose, Stephen E. *The Supreme Commander: The War Years of General Dwight D. Eisenhower*. New York: Doubleday, 1970.

Angelucci, Enzo. *Airplanes from the Dawn of Flight to the Present Day*. New York: McGraw-Hill, 1973.

Aron, Robert. *De Gaulle Before Paris: The Liberation of France, June–August 1944*. New York: Putnam, 1962.

Aster, Sidney. *1939: The Making of the Second World War*. New York: Simon and Schuster, 1974.

Baron, Richard; Baum, Abe; and Goldhurst, Richard. *Raid! The Untold Story of Patton's Secret Mission*. New York: Putnam, 1981.

Bauer, Eddy. *Illustrated World War II Encyclopedia* (24 vols.). Monaco: Jaspard Polus, 1966. English translation printed in the United States by H. S. Stuttman, Inc.

Bazna, Elyesa. *I Was Cicero*. New York: Harper & Row, 1962.

Bekker, Cajus. *The Luftwaffe War Diaries*. New York: Doubleday, 1968.

——. *Hitler's Naval War*. New York: Doubleday, 1974.

Belote, James H., and Belote, William M. *Corregidor: The Saga of a Fortress*. New York: Harper & Row, 1967.

Blair, Clay, Jr. *Silent Victory*. New York: Lippincott, 1975.

Boyington, Gregory. *Baa Baa Black Sheep*. New York: Putnam, 1958.

Bradley, Omar N. *A Soldier's Story*. New York: Henry Holt, 1951.

Brown, Anthony Cave. *Bodyguard of Lies*. New York: Harper & Row, 1975.

Buchanan, A. Russell. *The United States and World War II*. New York: Harper & Row, 1964.

Bullock, Alan. *Hitler — A Study in Tyranny*. New York: Harper & Row, 1963.

Butcher, Harry. *My Three Years with Eisenhower*. New York: Simon and Schuster, 1946.

Calvocoressi, Peter, and Wint, Guy. *Total War*. New York: Pantheon, 1972.

Carell, Paul. *The Foxes of the Desert*. New York: Dutton, 1961.

Catton, Bruce. *The War Lords of Washington*. New York: Harcourt Brace, 1948.

Churchill, Winston S. *The Second World War*. Boston: Houghton Mifflin, 1948-53.

Clark, Alan. *Barbarossa: The Russian-German Conflict, 1941–1945*. New York: Morrow, 1965.

Collier, Basil. *Japan at War*. London: Sidgwick and Jackson, 1975.

Collins, Larry, and Lapierre, Dominique. *Is Paris Burning?* New York: Simon and Schuster, 1965.

Cortesi, Lawrence. *Operation Bismarck Sea*. Canoga Park, California: Major Books, 1977.

Daley, Robert. *An American Saga: Juan Trippe and His Pan American Empire*. New York: Random House, 1980.

Dean, John R. *The Strange Alliance: The Story of Our Efforts at Wartime Cooperation with Russia*. New York: Viking, 1947.

De Gaulle, Charles. *War Memoirs*. New York: Simon and Schuster, 1964.

Deighton, Len. *Blitzkrieg*. New York: Knopf, 1980.

Delmer, Sefton. *The Counterfeit Spy*. New York: Harper & Row, 1971.

Dissette, Edward, and Adamson, Hans Christian. *Guerrilla Submarines*. New York: Bantam Books, 1980.

Dulles, Allen W. *The Craft of Intelligence*. New York: Harper & Row, 1963.

——. *The Secret Surrender*. New York: Harper & Row, 1966.

Eisenhower, Dwight D. *Crusade in Europe*. New York: Avon, 1968.

Elson, Robert. *Prelude to War*. New York: Time/Life, 1976.

Epstein, Helen. *Children of the Holocaust*. New York: Putnam, 1979.

Essame, Hubert, and Belfield, E. M. G. *Normandy Bridgehead*. New York: Ballantine, 1970.

Farago, Ladislas. *The Broken Seal*. New York, Random House, 1967.

——. *The Game of the Foxes*. New York: McKay, 1971.

Fleming, Peter. *Operation Sea Lion*. New York: Simon and Schuster, 1957.

Ford, Corey. *Donovan of OSS*. Boston: Little, Brown, 1970.

Friedheim, Eric and Taylor, Samuel W. *Fighters Up*. Philadelphia: Macrae-Smith, 1945.

Fuller, J. F. C. *The Second World War, 1939-1945*. New York: Duell, Sloan & Pearce, 1949.

Gavin, James M. *On to Berlin*. New York: Viking, 1978.

Goebbels, Joseph. *Diaries of Joseph Goebbels, 1942-1943*. New York: Doubleday, 1948.

Goralski, Robert. *World War II Almanac, 1939-1945*. New York: Putnam, 1981.

Hirsch, Phil. *War*. New York: Pyramid Books, 1964.

Hughes, Terry, and Costello, John. *The Battle of the Atlantic*. New York: Dial, 1977.

Innis, W. Joe, with Bunton, Bill. *In Pursuit of the Awa Maru*. New York: Bantam Books, 1981.

Irving, David. *The German Atomic Bomb*. New York: Simon and Schuster, 1968.

——. *The Trail of the Fox*. New York: Dutton, 1977.

Jackson, Stanley. *The Savoy: The Romance of a Great Hotel*. London: Frederick Muller, 1964.

Jackson, W. G. F. *The Battle for Italy*. London: Batsford, 1967.

Johnson, Frank D. *United States PT Boats of World War II*. Poole, Dorset, U.K.: Blandford Press, 1980.

Kahn, David, *The Codebreakers*. New York: Macmillan, 1967.

Kaufman, Louis; Fitzgerald, Barbara; and Sewell, Tom. *Mo Berg: Athlete, Scholar, Spy*. Boston: Little, Brown, 1974.

Keegan, John. *Who Was Who in World War II*. New York: Thomas Y. Crowell, 1978.

Keil, Sally Van Wagenen. *Those Wonderful Women in Their Flying Machines*. New York: Rawson, Wade, 1979.

Kimmel, Husband E. *Admiral Kimmel's Story*. Chicago: Henry Regnery, 1955.

King, Ernest J., and Whitehill, W. M. *Fleet Admiral King*. New York: Norton, 1952.

Kitchen, Ruben P., Jr. *Pacific Carrier*. New York: Zebra Books, 1980.

Kowalski, Isaac. *A Secret Press in Nazi Europe*. New York: Shengold, 1978.

Kramarz, Joachim. *Stauffenberg: The Life and Death of an Officer*. London: Deutsch, 1967.

Kurzman, Dan. *The Race for Rome*. New York: Doubleday, 1975.

Lawson, Ted W. *Thirty Seconds over Tokyo*. New York: Random House, 1943.

Leahy, W. I. *I Was There*. New York: Whittlesey, 1950.

Le Vien, Jack, and Lord, John. *Winston Churchill: The Valiant Years*. New York: Bernard Geis, 1962.

Lewin, Ronald. *The American Magic*. New York: Farrar, Straus & Giroux, 1982.

Longmate, Norman. *If Britain Had Failed*. New York: Stein & Day. 1974.

Lord, Walter. *Day of Infamy*. New York: Henry Holt, 1957.

——. *Incredible Victory*. New York: Harper & Row, 1967.

McClendon, Dennis E. *The Lady Be Good*. Fallbrook, Calif. (reprinted): Aero Publishers, Inc., 1982.

McKee, Alexander. *Last Round Against Rommel*. New York: New American Library, 1964.

Manchester, William. *American Caesar: Douglas MacArthur, 1880-1964*. Boston: Little, Brown, 1978.

Manvell, Roger, and Fraenkel, Heinrich. *The Canaris Conspiracy*. New York: McKay, 1969.

Marshall, Samuel. *Night Drop*. Boston: Little, Brown, 1962.

Mason, David. *Who's Who in World War II*. Boston: Little, Brown, 1978.

——. *U-Boat: The Secret Menace*. New York: Ballantine, 1968.

Michel, Henri. *The Shadow War*. New York: Harper & Row, 1973.

Michel, Jean. *Dora: The Nazi Concentration Camp Where Modern Space Technology Was Born and 30,000 Prisoners Died*. New York: Holt, Rinehart and Winston, 1980.

Mikesh, Robert C. *Japan's World War II Balloon Bomb Attacks on North America*. Washington: Smithsonian Institution Press, 1973.

Mollo, Andrew. *A Pictorial History of the SS*. New York: Bonanza, 1979.

Montagu, Ewen. *The Man Who Never Was*. Philadelphia: Lippincott, 1954.

Morella, Joe; Epstein, Edward Z.; and Griggs, John. *The Films of World War II*. New York: Citadel/Lyle Stuart, 1975.

Morison, Samuel E. *The History of United States Naval Operations in World War II* (14 vols.). Boston: Little, Brown, 1947–62.

Murphy, Robert. *Diplomat Among Warriors*. New York: Doubleday, 1964.

Page, Geoffrey. *Tale of a Guinea Pig*. New York: Bantam, 1981.

Patton, George S., Jr. *War As I Knew It*. Boston: Houghton Mifflin, 1947.

Payne, Robert. *The Life and Death of Adolf Hitler*. New York: Praeger, 1973.

Pearcy, Arthur. *DC-3*. New York: Ballantine, 1975.

Peniakoff, Vladimir. *Popski's Private Army*. New York: Bantam, 1980.

Popov, Dusko. *Spy-Counterspy*. New York: Grosset & Dunlap, 1974.

Preston, Antony. *Aircraft Carriers*. New York: Grosset & Dunlap, 1979.

Rayner, D. C. *Escort*. London: William Kimber and Company, 1955.

Ryan, Cornelius. *The Longest Day*. New York: Simon and Schuster, 1959.

——. *A Bridge Too Far*. New York: Simon and Schuster, 1974.

——. *The Last Battle*. New York: Simon and Schuster, 1966.

Schaeffer, Heinz. *U-Boat 977*. New York: Norton, 1953.

Sherrod, Robert. *Tarawa*. New York: Duell, Sloan & Pearce. 1944.

Shirer, William L. *The Rise and Fall of the Third Reich*. New York: Simon and Schuster, 1960.

Simms, Edward H. *American Aces*. New York: Harper & Brothers, 1958.

Speer, Albert. *Inside the Third Reich*. New York: Avon, 1970.

Stagg, J. M. *Forecast for Overload*. New York: Norton, 1972.

Steichen, Edward. *U.S. Navy War Photographs*. New York: Crown Publishers, 1956–1980.

Strong, Sir Kenneth. *Intelligence at the Top*. New York: Doubleday, 1969.

Sulzberger, C. L. *The American Heritage Picture History of World War II*. New York: American Heritage, 1966.

Sunderman, James F. *World War II in the Air*. New York: Franklin Watts, 1962.

TerHorst, Jerald F., and Albertazzie, Ralph. *The Flying White House*. New York: Coward, McCann & Geoghegan, 1979.

Thomson, David. *Europe Since Napoleon*. New York: Knopf, 1960.

Toland, John. *The Last 100 Days*. New York: Random House, 1965.

——. *The Rising Sun*. New York: Simon and Schuster, 1971.

Townsend, Peter. *Duel of Eagles*. New York: Simon and Schuster, 1971.

Tregaskis, Richard. *Guadalcanal Diary*. New York: Random House, 1943.

Truman, Harry S. *Memoirs*. New York: Doubleday, 1958.

Whiting, Charles. *Hitler's Werewolves*. New York: Bantam, 1973.

——. *The Hunt for Martin Bormann*. New York: Ballantine, 1973.

——. *Patton*. New York: Ballantine, 1971.

Wiener, Jan G. *The Assassination of Heydrich*. New York: Pyramid, 1969.

Williams, Eric. *The Wooden Horse*. New York: Bantam, 1980.

Winterbotham, Frederick W. *The Ultra Secret*. New York: Harper & Row, 1974.

Young, Desmond. *Rommel, the Desert Fox*. New York: Harper & Brothers, 1950.

Index